MAFIA BAGMAN

The Life and Times of a DC Mobster

ANGELO PARISI

Dedication

To the men and women of the Metropolitan Police Department
District of Columbia

Acknowledgments

For their help in making this project possible, I would like to thank the following colleagues who dealt with Joe Nesline earlier in their careers. FBI Special Agent Daniel A. Reilly, Detectives Karl N. Milligan of Prince George's County, Maryland Police Department Intelligence Unit and Carl M. Shoffler of the D.C. Metropolitan Police Department. Daniel Reilly is retired from the Bureau and is an author and professor of Criminology, Law, and Society at George Mason University. Karl Milligan is now retired and is president of his own Investigative / Consulting and Intelligence firm. Carl Shoffler, who passed-away in 1996, was best known for his participation in the arrest of the five people involved in the infamous 1972 "third-rate burglary," the Watergate scandal. After he retired from MPDC, he served with the Prince George's County, Maryland Fire Department (PGFD), where he was their chief intelligence officer and arson investigator. Anyone visiting Shoffler at his office would find him constantly on the phone maintaining his contacts with law enforcement colleagues, confidential sources as well as with the authors of many of the books that lined his office shelves.

I would also like acknowledge the love and support of my family. To my oldest, my daughter Angie who is very special and keeps me on the "Straight and Narrow." To my Firefighter son, Joseph "Easy" Parisi, who is also a very fine graphic designer, as evidenced by the excellent design of this book cover. To my youngest son and my editor Danny, who is a Senior Reporter for an on-line magazine and an author himself. And last but not least, to my wife Christina, the best sounding board and research assistant any aspiring author could have.

CONTENTS

Epilogue
"I thought we'd be dead by now"

I. A Tribute

Gambling and prostitution have been part of the underworld scene in Washington City since the beginning of the Republic

The Metropolitan Police Department of the District of Columbia (MPDC) was established in 1861 by Act of Congress. On March 19, 1911 an article appeared in the Washington Post newspaper written in tribute to Francis M. Doyle, the first D.C. police officer killed in the line of duty on December 29, 1871. The article which was transcribed by David Richardson (MPDC Ret.) can be found in its entirety on the website of the Metropolitan Police Department. The following is a summary of that article:

In post-civil war Washington City lawlessness prevailed in many sections, particularly in the Southwest section. At this time the area was inundated with hundreds of gambling houses, policy shops, lottery games, and disorderly houses, the proprietors of which openly violated the license laws. This area in fact was a hotbed of all kinds of crime and class of criminal. Among those who inhabited the area was the "Queen of Louse Alley" Mrs. John Shea. For years Mrs. Shea operated a brothel and gambling house on Maryland Avenue.

After weeks of effort an arrest warrant was issued for Mrs. Shea. The duty of executing the warrant was entrusted to Sergeant E.J. Duvall and Private Francis M. Doyle. Early in the evening the two men set out for Mrs. Shea's home. They calmly knocked at the front door and awaited her. A maid answered, and upon their request to see Mrs. Shea they were shown into a parlor. Mrs. Shea entered the room and welcomed the officers and inquired as to the nature of their visit with a smile that belied her real feeling. The woman was described as tall and beautiful, with a commanding figure.

Sergeant Duvall told the woman that she must accompany them to the station house. She agreed and rose to excuse herself to gather her wrap. The woman's suspicion was aroused, when Sergeant Duvall turned to Private Doyle and asked him to place her in handcuffs. Mrs. Shea slowly moved to the other side of the room, until she stood before an old-fashioned square piano by the wall. Private Doyle took a few steps to the side of Mrs. Shea. As she stood there one hand wandered to the top of the piano and into a slight recess between two pillows one hand closed around the grip of a heavy revolver.

Suddenly the woman whipped her right arm forward. A flash of flame, a puff of smoke, a report, and Private Doyle sank slowly to the floor. In a moment Sergeant Duvall had the woman within his grasp and wrested the empty gun from her hand and with a savage brutality pressed the handcuff about the murdering hand.

The police and surgeons from the hospital were ordered. Private Doyle was placed upon a mattress, his wound examined, and then for three hours the surgeons labored to keep alive the spark of life that could be barely detected. It was a vain task. Finally, death came, and blue coated men, who had stood shoulder to shoulder with Private Doyle in duty, reverently lifted his body and bore it to the home of the sorrowing family. Three days later he was buried. A whole city did him honor, and laid upon his grave their tribute of love and affection.

There is something inexpressibly sad about the history of that night. Upon Christmas day, Private Doyle was in his home taking toys from a tree for his children. Happy with his wife and family, he could have had no thought that so soon afterward the joy of the holiday season would be dimmed for all the city and to his family made deepest sorrow through his own death.

6

Memorial to Francis M. Doyle
Officer Killed in the Line of Duty
End of Watch: December 29, 1871
Rank: Officer Badge No. 48
Age: 38
Years of Service: Five
<u>Marital Status</u>: Married
<u>Children</u>: Three
Location of Death: 329 Maryland Avenue, S.W.

Officer Doyle was an Irish immigrant and like many police officers was a military veteran. He fought for the Union during the Civil war. Officer Francis Doyle's son, Robert Emmet Doyle, born in 1871, served 39 years on the D.C. Police Department and attained the rank of Captain.

II. INTRODUCTION

In 1979, I joined the Metropolitan Police Department of the District of Columbia (MPDC). During the crack cocaine epidemic of the 1980s and 1990s, the majority of my police work dealt with the crimes associated with the drug trade, especially the violent rivalries between neighborhood gangs or "Crews" as they were referred to in the District. I also participated in various gambling, prostitution and bootlegging cases, including an FBI case in the mid 1990s of an illegal sports betting operation connected to the New York Gambino Crime Family. While on the department I heard stories from senior officers and detectives about old time hustlers and gamblers from the 1930s into the 1970s with Mafia connections operating in the Washington metropolitan area. The most notable was D.C. gambling Kingpin Joe Nesline. Joe was mostly affiliated with the New York Genovese Crime Family. In the 1980s, Nesline was in his 70s and his name was still in the news for his run-ins with the criminal justice system in the District of Columbia and Florida.

The Mafia and the "Black Hand" had been present in America since the first wave of Sicilian and Southern Italian immigrants to New Orleans and New York City in the 1890s. But what we know as traditional Organized Crime in America as it existed from the end of the Prohibition Era in 1933 until the beginning of the 21st century, was set up by the "Father of Organized Crime" Charles "Lucky" Luciano and by the powerful Jewish mobster Meyer Lansky. They set up an organization composed mainly of Italian and Jewish factions known as the Commission and the Syndicate. This agreement of mutual respect was formalized at the Franconia Hotel in Manhattan in November of 1931. "Bugsy" Seigel reputedly stated "The yids and the dagos will no longer fight each other". Luciano set up the Commission to serve as the governing body for organized criminal factions. It was designed to decide which "Crime Family" controlled which territories and to settle all disputes. The Commission eventually came to be composed of the Five New York Crime Families, the Chicago Outfit and Crime Families from Buffalo, Miami, New Orleans, Los Angeles, Philadelphia, Detroit and Kansas City. The Mafia Family that "Lucky" Luciano took over became the Luciano Crime Family which eventually became the Genovese Family. The Syndicate involved both Italian, Jewish and other ethnic factions with the Commission having the last word on all major decisions. Together, these two criminal governing bodies will be referred to as the "Mob."

The Damon Runyonesque character Joseph Francis "Possum" Nesline and his Mob partner Charles "The Blade" Tourine were the connection between the District of Columbia and the Mob. They were the Syndicate's bag-men in the Washington, D.C. Metropolitan area. Their connection to the Commission and the Syndicate was through the Genovese Family. Charlie Tourine and Joe Nesline also looked after the interests of other Mafia families in New Jersey and Miami which included gambling operations in the Caribbean and on both sides of the Atlantic. Nesline's criminal activities were primarily gambling and prostitution. He was also involved in pornography, narcotics trafficking and the fight game.

As a fan of old movies especially the post-war Film Noirs of the 40s and 50s, the thought of mobsters like Joe Nesline operating in the District of Columbia intrigued me. After my retirement I began to research the times and the crimes surrounding Nesline, his associates and his connections. During my research, one name came up that I was familiar with, Langhorne "Lang" Carter Rorer. In September of 1990, I was involved in a joint FBI/MPDC investigation. The case concerned a D.C. Drug Crew responsible for multiple murders. The Crew dealt with two older "Old-School" D.C. hustlers who were their middlemen with national and international drug connections. One of those middlemen was the Crew's heroin connection, Lang Rorer who at the time was in his late 70s. My research found that Lang Rorer was a contemporary of Nesline and also an associate in his gambling operations, specifically a floating craps game that Nesline ran between Maryland, the District of Columbia and into Virginia, all the while staying one step ahead of the Feds.

Nesline made his way up the criminal food chain via his close relationships with Meyer Lansky and Charlie Tourine. Because he wasn't of Italian descent, he could never be a "Made-Guy" in the Mafia, however, his business acumen and legendary reputation for running the most profitable dice game on the East Coast allowed him to rise in status and become D.C.'s only true criminal Mob chief. According to his FBI file, Nesline maintained a wide network of gangland connections and extensive gambling interests in Cuba, the Bahamas, Europe and the Middle East, most ventures being financed by Lansky and Tourine.

In the early 20th century gambling was an adventure, and for guys like Joe Nesline a way of attaining class. As young men they lived by their wits and moved in unscrupulous and violent circles. Good gamblers possessed a head for numbers. They usually had very little formal education and some were illiterate. However, most could mentally perform elaborate mathematical calculations and more importantly, they could figure out odds and payoffs on the spot. In those days, gambling wasn't placing bets with On-Line Sports Books or putting money into the "One-Armed Bandits" of today's legalized casinos, it was dealing with real bandits with guns and brass knuckles. Gamblers literally played at their own risk. This was the world that old-school Washington, D.C. gamblers and hustlers operated in. There were other mobsters who were contemporaries of Nesline operating in the District's metropolitan area who were associated with elements of Traditional Organized Crime, but Joe Nesline was the most unique and notorious. His associations and business dealings both legal and illegal involved a Who's-Who of the underworld and the over-world around the world.

1

"The Bag Man"

Joseph Francis Nesline

Joe Nesline at his indictment for his gambling operation

at the Sportsman Club 1963

(photo Tampamafia.com)

Joe Nesline was born in Washington, D.C. in 1913 and grew up around 6th & Massachusetts Avenue, N.E. He dropped out of Gonzaga Catholic High School, and like many of his teenaged contemporaries, Joe started running liquor during prohibition. He brought rye and bourbon from the stills of southern Maryland into the District for the "Foggy Bottom Gang" which was led by the Warring brothers. Joe was especially close to the middle brother, Emmet "Little Man" Warring. At $50 to $100 a trip, it was a lucrative business although a dangerous

11

one. On one of his liquor runs Joe crashed a car full of booze in a high-speed chase and sustained serious head trauma. He did not receive the proper medical treatment at the time, and later he developed epilepsy requiring medication to control his seizures. He would periodically fall into uncontrollable fits of rage, one of which was a violent jealous assault on his second wife Josephine Alvarez that eventually led to their divorce.

Joe spent his young adulthood in the Ohio River town of Steubenville, where he hung out at the cigar shops that were fronts for illegal gambling operations up until Las Vegas gambling became legal in 1931. While working at Steubenville's most well-known gambling establishment, Rex's Cigar Store, Joe associated with future famous personalities in the gambling and entertainment world. Dean Martin, the most famous son of Steubenville got his start as a croupier at Rex's Cigar Store back when he was known as Dino Paul Crochetti.

Joe rubbed elbows with sports commentator and Las Vegas bookmaker "Jimmy the Greek" (Dimetrios Georgios Synodinos). But Joe's closest friend from Steubenville was Dino Cellini. Both Joe and Dino would later go on to work together for the "Gentleman Gambler" James "Jimmy" LaFontaine who operated the Maryland Athletic Club, better known as "Jimmy's Place," an illegal gambling establishment just across the Washington, D.C. border in Bladensburg, Maryland.

The Mafia's incursion into the District's criminal underworld was more gradual and discreet then in other cities. No city of importance was left out of the clutches of the Mob. It was inconceivable to mobsters like Frank Costello in New York and Charlie Fischetti in Chicago that a rich, important center like Washington, D.C. could be bypassed. After prohibition in the District of Columbia the rackets were dominated by local racketeers like Jimmy La Fontaine, the Warring brothers, Roger "Whitetop" Simpkins, Abe "Jew Boy" Deitz, William "Snags" Lewis and others. They staked out locations in Washington and worked together in harmony, well aware that the authorities in the nation's capital would not go for the violence and gun play of Chicago and New York.

The Syndicate avoided hands-on operations in the District, however, some outside mobsters did try some of the same tactics in the District they used to muscle in on the local underworld in other towns. By the 1940s, after a rash of robberies of local underworld figures, the District's racketeers saw the light and made their peace with the Mob. The local operators retained nominal control of vice, gambling, narcotics, and bootleg liquor and paid tribute to the Syndicate. As a result of Joe Nesline honing his practical skills earlier in Mob controlled Steubenville and at Jimmy's Place in Maryland, and his association with Dino Cellini, the Mob and in particular Meyer Lansky placed Joe as overseer of gambling operations in the Washington metropolitan area.

In 1951, Joe became infamous after he shot and killed another gambler in a Georgetown "Bottle Club" in front of onlookers, some of whom supported Joe's claim of self-defense. He hired the best criminal defense lawyers in D.C. at the time, and won an acquittal of the murder charge, although he was convicted of illegal possession of a firearm. The year Joe served on that gun charge was his only prison sentence for an adult criminal conviction, though in 1981 he did languish for some months in a Miami jail on a contempt-of-court charge. This was as a result of refusing to testify before a grand jury in a civil case involving U.S. federal judge Alcee Hastings (later Congressman Hastings of Florida).

Joe was the king of local gambling, with numerous clubs in the District and suburban Maryland. The Maryland club was named "George Raft's Rendezvous" for the popular 1940s actor, George Raft who was the host of the club. Joe ran casinos in Cuba for Meyer Lansky and Santo Trafficante Jr. and worked with the Genovese family in Europe. He considered himself to be the best craps-shooter and craps-dealer in the world, or so he bragged during an FBI interview. He also admitted to being involved in professional sports betting with Las Vegas handicappers to set odds and point spreads.

In 1966 Joe married and traveled the world with his second wife a former "Burlesque Queen" Josephine Alvarez whose stage name was "Sofina." Josephine was born in 1941 in New York City to Columbian immigrant parents. In 2009, she wrote a book titled "Lucky '325'" detailing her life and her time with Joe and his Mob associates. A second woman in Joe's life was another burlesque performer named Erica "Heidi" Rikan aka "Kathie Deiter." Heide was Joe Nesline's money courier for his various enterprises around the world. She was also a Madam who gained notoriety for her involvement in the Watergate scandal.

14

In the historical fiction novel about the Watergate affair titled "City of Shadows" published in 2000, the pseudonymous author James Dalton portrays Joe Nesline as the murderous D.C. Mob boss "Joseph R. Nezneck." The Madam in the Watergate scandal, Heidi Rikan is referred to as "Heidi Ryker." Other characters from Nesline's life and times also make their appearance in Dalton's novel.

While newspapers designated Nesline as "The Boss of D.C." and alleged that he had ties to New York's Genovese crime family, Joe Nesline maintained he was an honest gambler and gaming consultant. He maintained that his tables were fair and he paid off when he lost. Joe loved high stakes play at one-on-one card games and craps, but he also bet on sports and just about anything else. He was local, and although his business interests were international, his base was the District of Columbia, where he was known and felt comfortable.

The following testimony is an excerpt from the September, 1973 Organized Crime hearings before the Permanent Subcommittee on Investigations of the United States Senate, 93rd Congress. The witness is a Mafia associate, Louis Pasquale Mastriana who was being questioned on his knowledge of organized crime:

"From the outset, I have been directly involved in crimes involving stolen securities, fraudulent or worthless securities and the cashing of completely worthless offshore, and foreign bank instruments which were designed to defraud banks and other investors.

During the war years I went to work at an Arsenal. One of the reasons for leaving the Arsenal was I suffered a gunshot wound. I was shot in the chest in a bar called the Jungle Inn after heisting a crap game in Albany, NY.

I was becoming involved in organized crime activities, especially in the field of gambling. I then migrated back to the Bronx in New York with my mother. While I was there, I went to work for a person known as "Jimmy Blue Eyes," Vincent Alo. I picked up the numbers lottery for "Jimmy Blue Eyes," and I went out and collected some bad debts. Since that time, Vincent Alo has become a powerful organized crime figure.

Then. later on, through people in Manhattan, I went to work for Joe Nesline who at that time was working for Charlie "The Blade" Tourine. Nesline was turning numbers money in to Tourine and Tourine was working for the Genovese people in New York. I went to work for Joe Nesline here in Washington, D.C. as a runner, picking up numbers and I also picked up his bad debts, what is commonly referred to possibly as an enforcer.

In 1945, I left D.C. and went to work at the Naval Supply Depot in Oklahoma as a truck driver. From there I migrated to Hot Springs, Arkansas, I went to work for Owney Madden who operated several gambling establishments in that city.

In about 1947, I returned to Washington, D.C., again going to work for Joe Nesline. During the course of working for Nesline, I got myself involved in a situation where I received some stolen government checks. I served 3 to 15 months sentence at Lorton, Va. In 1949, I went to the Atlanta Penitentiary to serve a 21 to 63 months sentence for passing stolen government checks."

As a side note, during the same 1973 Senate hearings while under oath, Louis Mastriana stated he was instrumental in foiling a 1968 assassination attempt on the Bahamian Prime Minister. Elliott Roosevelt, the son of former president Franklin Roosevelt, was accused of involvement in the plot. In 1968, Elliott Roosevelt and an alleged mobster front man, Michael J. McLaney, offered Louis Mastriana $100,000 to assassinate Prime Minister Lynden Pindling. Mastriana was paid $10,800 up front, most of which came from Roosevelt. The check to pay Mastriana was signed by Elliott Roosevelt. The assassination plot was conceived after Prime Minister Pindling's failure to issue a gambling license to an associate of Meyer Lansky, whom Michael J. McLaney worked for. It was uncovered by Mastriana; he taped all of his conversation with Elliott Roosevelt, allegedly using equipment from the U.S. Postal Inspectors Service. Roosevelt maintained that this was a lie until his death.

In the mid 1960s, Joe attempted to go legit by partnering with Charlie Tourine and entering into a wig business in the District. The Securities and Exchange Commission (SEC) nixed that endeavor. The Feds believed the business to be a

17

front for gambling and cocaine trafficking due to the wig company's manager Gabriel "Gabby" Bobrow, a convicted narcotics trafficker.

Joseph Nesline, as an "Associate" of the Mob, was being groomed to replace Meyer Lansky as the Mob's money handler. Joe was not of Italian descent he needed a "Made Man" as a partner, just like Lansky needed Vincent 'Jimmy Blue Eyes" Alo as his partner and protector. And like his Mob associates, Joe was hounded by the Feds and local law enforcement from D.C. to the Caribbean to Europe.

2

"The Made Man"

Charles Tourine

Charles "The Blade" Tourine aka Charlie White

(Photo The BUTTONGUYS / The New York Mafia)

Charles "The Blade" Tourine aka Charlie White was placed in the role of partner and protector for Joe Nesline by the Syndicate. Tourine was born in 1906 in Matawan, New Jersey. He earned his ominous handle for the way he dealt with debtors who refused to pay and tough guys who stood in his way. He combined a penchant for violence with a knack for gambling. Though illiterate, he would go on to run casinos in Cuba, Las Vegas, and Europe. Tourine was one of the original members of the American Mafia at its inception during the Prohibition Era.

As a young man Charlie Tourine began his career as a "torpedo" (a strong-arm) working with a New Jersey-based Luciano crew led by Ruggerio "Richard" Boiardo aka "The Boot." Informants alleged Charlie was a gunman/executioner, traveling throughout the states as asked, to eliminate various problems. He racked up dozens of arrests ranging from rum-running to murder and served time in several federal and state penitentiaries. As his career progressed, he evolved into a top hoodlum. His specialty became varied gambling operations, illegal craps games and lay-off services in New Jersey, Miami and Washington, D.C. He was also involved in legitimate financial investments in legalized casinos throughout the world.

Even though Charlie was identified as a Capo with the Genovese Crime Family in New York, he was still an enigma. He was one of the most independent Mafioso to ever operate in the states. He was associated with Santo Trafficante Jr. of Tampa and traveled extensively looking out for the Genovese and Trafficante interests in Cuba and South Florida. Charlie ran gambling concessions at resort hotels in Miami and Palm Beach for Ruggerio "The Boot" Boiardo. His personal "crew" of hoodlum associates included several non-Italians like his close friend, Joe Nesline, who was the top gambling mechanic in Tourine's crew. Charlie was Nesline's connection to gangsters like Meyer Lansky and "Lucky" Luciano. Charlie and Joe had known each other since the 1940s. While Joe worked the numbers operation in D.C. with Emmitt "Little Man" Warring, a cut of the action went to Charlie Tourine. They would go on to run strip clubs and illegal gambling operations in Washington, D.C. and Maryland. In 1951, Tourine was included on a government list of 126 notorious underworld figures whose income taxes were being investigated.

Charlie resided in some of the most exclusive neighborhoods in Manhattan, Miami and Havana. His main base of operation was an apartment on Central Park South, one of the wealthiest sections of New York City. During a New York State legislative hearing on crime, Charlie was asked how he could afford his Central Park residence. Charlie stated he had his own money that he did not keep in banks, "the last time I did the federal government took it." When asked where he kept his money, Charlie responded "Behind bricks, in cans." He refused to divulge how much money he did have stating, "That's my business." He spent his winters in Florida at the Beaux Arts Apartments in Miami where he partnered with Nesline in a bookmaking lay-off operation. He also maintained a residence at the exclusive Harbor Island in Miami Beach.

In November 1955, Santo Trafficante Jr. opened the Hotel Capri and the Sans Souci Hotels in Havana, Cuba. The Salon Rojo Casino in the Hotel Capri was run by Charlie Tourine, Joe Nesline and other New York mobsters. The actor George Raft was the public face of the Hotel Capri's Casino. Tourine was connected with Cuban strongman General Fulgencio Batista and his business associate Roberto "Chiri" Mendoza, a wealthy Cuban contractor and sugar planter. Mendoza was Batista's liaison to the American Mafia gamblers. In 1958, Conrad Hilton opened the Hotel Tryp Habana in Havana with great fanfare and five days of star-studded celebrations. The casino in the hotel was leased for $1 million a year to a group consisting of Roberto "Chiri" Mendoza, Clifford "Big Juice" Jones and others. Clifford Jones was the former Lieutenant Governor of Nevada.

In his 2013 book, author Jack Colhoun coined the term "Gangsterismo," (the title of the book) for the Mob's influence in Havana. The era of Gangsterismo in Cuba came to an end when Fidel Castro's "July 26th Movement" revolutionaries triumphed over Batista on New Year's Day 1959. On January 8, during a television interview broadcast in New York, Castro vowed to "clean out all gamblers who used the influence of Dictator Batista's regime to build an empire here." Nesline was part of the exodus of North American gamblers out of Cuba. According to an FBI report, Tourine remained in Cuba until mid-1959, moving "bags of money out of Cuba following the takeover by Castro." Most of that money belonging to Santo Trafficante Jr. Tourine was arrested by Cuban authorities along with Trafficante, Meyer Lansky's brother Jake Lansky, and other Mafia gamblers. Tourine was detained briefly and was deported in June 1959. When the Mob lost control of Havana after Castro's revolution, Charlie Tourine became a public relations advance man in efforts by the Havana Mob to establish a web of contacts throughout the Caribbean.

In 1965, a confidential FBI informant advised the Bureau that Charlie Tourine was suspected of being present at the infamous Mafia summit held at the estate of mobster Joseph "Joe the Barber" Barbara, in Apalachin, New York, on November 14, 1957. The historic Summit of the American Mafia held in upstate New York was hosted by Joe Barbara, a Boss of the Bufallino crime family. The meeting was called by Vito Genovese to discuss who would assume control of the illegal operations which had been controlled by the late Boss of the Gambino crime family, the "Lord High Executioner," Albert Anastasia, who was murdered in October 1957. Over 100 Mafiosi from the United States, Italy, and Cuba attended this meeting. After taking control of the Luciano Crime Family from Frank Costello, Vito Genovese renamed the family after himself. Frank Costello took over control of the Luciano family when "Lucky" was imprisoned and later deported to Italy after World War II. Costello never changed the name of the family. Vito wanted to legitimize his new power by holding a national Mob meeting. In 1958, Charlie Tourine was arrested on a weapons charge and questioned by the FBI about the murder of Albert Anastasia.

According to a CIA draft report Charlie "the Blade" Tourine, Santo Trafficante Jr., Sam Giancana, Johnny Roselli, Carlos Marcello and other Mob members participated in multiple CIA efforts to kill and/or overthrow Fidel Castro. In one of these attempts a girlfriend of Charlie Tourine, along with future Watergate burglar and Trafficante associate Frank Sturgis, unsuccessfully tried to poison Castro in Havana. Cuban-American Frank Sturgis (Frank Angelo Fiorini), was originally a member of Fidel Castro's revolutionary army but turned against him when Castro revealed himself to be a communist. These failed assassination efforts led to the disastrous "Bay of Pigs" invasion. Subsequent to his arrest for the Watergate break-in, Sturgis admitted to D.C. police detective Carl Shoffler that he was a Trafficante associate. According to an August 1976, House Select

Committee on Assassinations (HSCA) report Sturgis was also associated with both Joe Nesline and Charlie Tourine.

In 1968, New York Customs Agents uncovered crates of illegal pornographic magazines shipped from Copenhagen. The contraband was eventually traced to Tourine, who was subsequently indicted for conspiring to bribe customs agents in order to smuggle $250,000 worth of adult literature into the country. During the 1970 trial, all witnesses refused to answer questions, and no convictions were awarded.

According to a 1969 FBI report, Charlie Tourine interceded on behalf of New York Socialite Marietta Tree when she became indebted to a loan shark because of her excessive shopping habits. Not wanting her husband to know of her situation, in some unknown manner, Marietta made contact with Charlie Tourine. Tourine, together with Jilly Rizzo, who was Frank Sinatra's close friend, soon resolved the matter.

Marietta Endicott Peabody FitzGerald Tree was a Democratic Party activist. In 1960 she was appointed by President Kennedy as the United States Representative to the United Nations Commission on Human Rights. From 1938 to 1947 Marietta was married to New York lawyer Desmond FitzGerald. By the 1950s Desmond would become the Deputy Director of the CIA. At the time of her financial predicament Marietta was married to her second husband Anglo-

American aristocrat Arthur Tree. Their marriage lasted from 1947 until his death in 1976.

Marietta Tree at home in New York 1954

(photo credit Cecil Beaton)

Arthur Ronald Lambert Field Tree was a former British Member of Parliament from 1933 to 1945. His mother was Ethel Field, daughter of Marshal Field, founder of Chicago's Marshal Field Department store.   Ronald Tree's mother Ethel was what was known at the time as an "American Dollar Princess." In the late 19th century, wealthy American female socialites, known as "Dollar Princesses," began flocking to England and marrying cash strapped British aristocrats for a coveted noble title. This trend started in 1874, when American heiress Jennie Jerome married Lord Randolph Churchill. Their son, Winston Churchill, became Britain's war time Prime Minister. The trend continued until the end of World War II.

Marietta had affairs during both of her marriages. She had affairs with Hollywood director John Huston, American politician Adlai Stevenson and noted English architect and urban planner Richard Llewelyn-Davies. Marietta had bit parts in the 1960, John Huston film "The Misfits" and in the 1988, Danny Huston film "Mr. North." Danny Houston is John Huston's son.

In January 1970, the New York State Joint Legislative Committee on Crime was investigating the relationship between the motion picture industry and organized crime and also "the involvement of non-Italians in organized crime." During the committee hearings a tape recording was played of a conversation between Tourine and Kirk Kerkorian, the controlling stockholder of Metro-Goldwyn-Mayer studios and founding partner of the original MGM Hotel in Las Vegas. In a 1961 FBI recording, a voice identified as Charles Tourine was heard explaining to Kirkorian the best way to send him money. A check was to be given to movie star George Raft, who was to cash the check and deliver it to Tourine. All parties refused to answer questions. Tourine, who arrived at the hearing on crutches, invoked his Fifth Amendment right 50 times during the proceedings and no explanation was ever made as to what the monies were for. It was alleged that Tourine introduced a third-party to Kirkorian in order to finance the purchase by Kerkorian of a DC-8 airplane, then valued at 8 million dollars. The deal never came off.

In November 1970, Tourine was spotted several times having lunch with Frank Costello at Gatsby's Restaurant in New York City. These meetings, held after the death of Vito Genovese, led authorities to speculate that Costello was coaxed out of retirement to help sort out the family's transition. Charlie Tourine was being considered as a possible successor to Vito Genovese. The fact that Charlie was illiterate prevented the move.

In July 1976, the semi-retired Tourine moved to Miami, Florida, but he could never turn down a good business opportunity. In August of that year Tourine along with several former federal and state officials from Alaska pleaded innocent to federal charges stemming from a scheme to establish a gambling and prostitution ring along the new Alaskan pipeline. Dominick Santerelli of the Chicago Outfit and Phillip Damiano of the Cleveland Mob owned most of the land around the Alaskan port city of Valdez where the pipeline was being laid. Phill Damiano was murdered shortly before the trial was set to begin. After a lengthy trial, Tourine and the remaining five co-conspirators were eventually acquitted.

In 1977, Tourine was one of five high-level mobsters including Meyer Lansky, to be subpoenaed by Florida's Dade County State Attorney's office to answer questions about the May 1976 murder of former Mafioso Johnny Roselli, whose body was found stuffed in an oil drum in Biscayne Bay. Roselli had testified before several grand juries and committees about a plot by the CIA to kill Fidel Castro by recruiting the Mafia for the CIA's "Operation Mongoose." He was also questioned about his knowledge of the JFK assassination.

3

"In the Beginning"

The Numbers Game

The nation's capital is a city born and nurtured by a lottery

"All roads lead to Rome," but even in ancient times roads to the imperial capital city could not be maintained without spare denarii from the plebeians. After a civil war, Caesar Augustus instituted a lottery system to pay for repairs of the damaged infrastructure. America itself is the offspring of a lottery. In order to finance the privately-held Virginia Company of London, King James I granted the company the authority to hold a lottery to raise funds for a grand exposition. Proceeds from the lottery were used to create Jamestown in Virginia, the first English colony in the New World. After America's second war of Independence, the War of 1812, Congress approved a Grand National Lottery with a jackpot of $100,000. The profits of this were to be put towards restoring and expanding Washington City. After the winners were drawn the broker contracted to conduct the lottery absconded with the proceeds, never to be seen again. With such a history, it is no wonder that "the numbers game" became one of the biggest businesses in America's Capital City.

The numbers game started in the 1920s and was known as the "Italian Lottery," a numbers betting game played in the Italian immigrant enclaves. Laborers could bet as little as a penny on winning a three number combination. The daily winning numbers were published in newspapers in Italy where the lottery was legal. In 1958, Italian-American New Orleans bandleader and trumpet player, Louie "The Lip" Prima released an album titled "Breaking it up." One of the songs on the album is about a bookie named "Luigi." Louie Prima sings the song with an Italian accent. The last line of the song is, "My dear Paisanos, I'm-a-telling you. Don't be like Luigi, or da-policeman will get you, too!" The numbers racket, or the daily number soon expanded to other poor and working-class neighborhoods, especially in Italian American and African American communities in major cities across the United States.

As this form of illegal gambling or illegal lottery would come to be played, a bettor picks three digits to match those that would be randomly drawn the following day. For many years the "number" had been the last three digits of "the handle," the amount race track bettors placed on race day at a major racetrack. The results were then published in racing journals and major newspapers in New York City. Gamblers place bets with a bookmaker ("bookie") at a tavern, bar, barber shop, social club, or any other semi-private place that acts as an illegal betting parlor. Runners carry the money and betting slips between the betting parlors and the headquarters, called a numbers bank. The odds against winning at the numbers game were 999 to 1. As the game is usually played, the person who selects the winning number is paid 600 to 1, and the gross average profit of the promoters is nearly 40 percent of the amounts wagered. The inducement to the bettor is that a 10-cent risk may yield $60. The promoters and operators of numbers games routinely paid large sums to politicians and police to protect against arrest. In D.C. this protection money was known as "Ice." The amounts bet on numbers annually in the United States were estimated as high as hundreds of millions of dollars, although such figures were unverifiable.

In Washington, D.C., in the 1950s, the take from the numbers in pennies, nickels, dimes, and quarters, were deposited in the branch of the Hamilton bank at 20th and Pennsylvania Avenue N.W., in the Foggy Bottom section. A Congressional committee investigating local crime ascertained that the bank did not report the large deposits of small coins. The deposits were withdrawn each day and transferred to Maryland, where local bagmen for the syndicate divided the receipts and sent its cut to the Mafia in New York. Whenever the police did make an arrest of the numbers-runners, they were usually represented by a member of the Charlie Ford law firm, the same law firm that defended Joe Nesline during his murder trial.

"Lotteries are a tax laid on the willing only"
Thomas Jefferson

4

"The Oldest Profession"

Hooker's Brigade

In the 1800s, the stagecoaches which carried politicos to Washington City, the Territory of Columbia as it was then known, also brought the first "ladies of the evening." In the early days of the Republic, the city was inhabited almost entirely by lone men who whiled away their free time at cards and dice, making Washington a gambler's garden. Grifters and prostitutes flocked into the city and became an integral and important segment of the population. Prostitution flourished as an essential and honorable trade. Anti-prostitution laws were not enacted until the years between the two world wars, mostly to stop the spread of sexually transmitted diseases among the military.

During the Civil War following the Union Army's defeat at the First Battle of Bull Run, less than thirty miles from the Capital, Major General George B. McClellan assigned Brigadier General Joseph Hooker the task of protecting the President and defending Washington City from further Confederate incursions. Joseph "Fighting Joe" Hooker was a Regular Army veteran with a checkered reputation as a ladies-man with rumors of drunkenness that dogged him for much of his career. His headquarters were known for parties and gambling.

Hooker quickly established his encampment just outside the city as part of the effort to organize and train the new Army of the Potomac. He started to bring discipline to his demoralized command. However, in their off-duty hours his soldiers continued gambling, drinking and patronizing the growing numbers of prostitutes. McClellan ordered Hooker to get his men under control. Hooker was a veteran soldier with the same weakness of the flesh as his men. He knew it was impossible to eliminate prostitution, so his pragmatic solution was to contain it. He ordered the military police to move the city's prostitutes into an area south of Pennsylvania Avenue that had become an infamous slum known as "Murder Bay." This area was roughly bounded by Constitution Avenue, Pennsylvania Avenue and 15th Street, N.W. (the area currently known as Federal Triangle). The prostitutes that refused to relocate were subsequently loaded onto a waiting steamboat named the "Idahoe" and shipped off to the aptly named town of "Loveladies" New Jersey. The remaining prostitutes quickly took up residence in Murder Bay to serve the needs of the Army of the Potomac. The area soon became known as "Hooker's Division," and the prostitutes were referred to as "Hooker's Brigade." Though it's debatable this alone is responsible for the synonym "Hooker," it certainly helped to spread the term.

During his time as commander of the forces protecting Washington City, General Hooker was a secret and frequent guest at a large brothel known as "The Haystack," kept by Madam Bella Hay. The house, located on the northwest corner of Murder Bay, housed prostitutes and contained a large, lower-class gambling den known to almost every soldier. Madam Bella Hay was a woman with a history of providing female companions to the prominent men that frequented Washington City. Known only to a select few, Madam Hay was also loyal to the Confederacy and served as a spy for the South's Secret Service. Bella Hay was known by many colorful titles. The most socially acceptable one was "The Belle of the Shenandoah." Bella continued operating her prostitution empire long after the war ended. While the iconic Haystack was forced to close following General Hooker's departure, she opened up new, more sophisticated brothels such as "Hay's Private Residence for Ladies" and the "Velvet Cottage by the Sea." While on a speaking tour in 1889, she delivered dramatic lectures of her life as a Confederate spy and Madam.

Portrait of Madam Bella Hay ca. 1860
(photo RelicRecord)

The legacy of Madam Bella Hay lives on whenever someone enjoys a
"Roll in the Hay"

5

"Monte Carlo on the Potomac"

The rise and fall of the District's notorious sister-city,

"Jackson City," Virginia

"The Monte Carlo of America," the settlement featured all the ingredients of a memorable night on the town – saloons, gambling houses, bordellos, vice dens and race tracks

(photo Arlington Fire Journal & D.C. Fire History)

On February 27, 1801, Congress passed the District of Columbia Organic Act taking 69 square miles of territory from Maryland and taking 31 square miles from Virginia across the Potomac River which encompassed the port city of Alexandria. The 100 square mile territory was officially placed under the control of Congress

34

as the District of Columbia. From the moment of its passage, Virginia was looking for a way to get its territory back. It was not until the Alexandria Retrocession Act of 1846 that the land was returned to the State of Virginia.

In 1835, a group of New York speculators made plans for a new city on the Virginia side of the Potomac but within the boundary of the District of Columbia, located near what is now the Pentagon and Reagan National Airport. The investors believed the new city would transform the capital into one of the most prestigious cities in the world. Hoping for a grand founding ceremony, the New Yorkers set out to secure the participation of the "National Hero" and 7th President of the United States, Andrew Jackson. The New Yorkers turned on the charm and after receiving flattering letters from the investors Jackson agreed to the venture. They named the new city Jackson City in his honor.

"We are well aware that the enterprise as presented, does not exhibit a grandeur corresponding with the splendor of [your] name... [but we] feel sanguine that at no distant day JACKSON CITY will not be unworthy of its name. It has appeared to us also as peculiarly proper that the second man of the Union should have his name placed by the side of that of the first; we trust that, Jackson City will grow in happy union with Washington City ..."

On January 11, 1836, thousands of Washingtonians gathered to watch the Laying of the Cornerstone ceremony. Following a speech by George Washington Parke Custis, the step-grandson of George Washington, President Andrew Jackson

35

placed a large elaborate cornerstone containing official documents, newspapers, coins, medals and other articles. A more fitting cornerstone ceremony occurred that same evening. Under the cover of darkness, a group of spectators returned to the site, broke into the cornerstone's capsule, and ran off with its contents. Jackson City would never achieve the status the speculators hoped for.

Jackson City was described as a "never-was-been" and the "invisible city." The city got its first taste of gambling after the Civil War when New Jersey investors moved in to escape anti-gambling laws in their home state. About the same time Congress began restricting gambling in Washington City. The District's gamblers abandoned their old haunts in D.C. and set up shop on the Virginia side of the Potomac River. Jackson City became most notable for horse-racing. The city had St. Asaph's Racetrack and Alexander Island Racetrack which is now one of the Pentagon's parking lots. The city also had telegraph wires running to tracks across the country.

Even though Jackson City was a favorite destination for many Washingtonians, it became too much for the locals. The city became known by another name, "Hell's Bottom." In his book "Wicked Northern Virginia," Michael Lee Pope, quoting Arlington historian Eleanor Lee Teleman, describes the effects the area's growing reputation had on crime:

"Northern Virginia was becoming the 'Monte Carlo of America,' a reputation that attracted violent criminals from Washington and Maryland. Gamblers in Jackson

City could lose money in all manner of ways; cards, craps, or roulette. Dangerous characters roamed the streets. Farmers returning home from market traveled in packs to avoid being robbed by highwaymen. Killings were commonplace, and cases were never brought to trial."

In February 1896, Alexandria Deputy Sheriff Edward Deuterman took it upon himself to clean up the town. He formed a posse with a friend and eight local black men and raided a specific gambling saloon. What was supposed to be a quick raid ended in a hail of gunfire. Deuterman and his friend were wounded, another in his posse was killed and four others wounded. The raid became the catalyst for a long and drawn-out war against vice in Alexandria which took nearly a dozen more years to win. Any justice for the wounded and killed was slow and ultimately lost.

Jackson City was also a fire-trap and District of Columbia firefighters frequently responded to the city to douse the flames of the gambling houses. The shops were repaired - and the games resumed.

Fire visited Jackson City on November 30, 1893, and the next day's Washington Post said:

``Monte Carlo, the notorious resort at Jackson City, is in ashes. About 11:30 o'clock last night fire broke out in one of the rows of frame buildings occupied by the free and easy, and before the flames could be checked almost the entire row was destroyed."

On July 14, 1902, flames again swept a row of card parlors, as The Washington Post reported:

``Fire that originated in a policy shop last night wiped out every gambling house in Jackson City, at the Virginia end of the Long Bridge. It was not much of a fire when it started - a bucketful of water would have quenched it - but the habitues were so absorbed at the roulette wheel and faro table that they refused to put out the blaze.''

In 1892, Virginia's Assembly had passed a bill banning all forms of gambling except horseracing (possibly due to the fact that some State Senators were primary investors in the racetracks). In spite of this bill, those in power continued to receive kickbacks from the gambling operators and the ban went un-enforced, until Crandal Mackey, a progressive Alexandria County Attorney General came on the scene and was determined to clean up Jackson City.

Crandal Mackey joined a faction known as the "Progressives," an anti-corruption party. Mackey's aim was to consolidate the progressive movement's hold over Alexandria County. At this time the temperance movement joined with the progressive movement and made a strong case for the prohibition of alcohol. Gambling and drunkenness were seen to go hand in hand and Jackson City abounded with both. In 1903, Crandal was elected Alexandria County Attorney General by a narrow margin and set his sights on the elimination of gambling in northern Virginia.

On May 30th, Memorial Day 1904, a group of civilians led by Mackey boarded a train from Washington to Arlington. His group of civic crusaders, whom he had just sworn in as official deputies of the County, were called the "Good Citizens League." Upon arrival in Jackson City, Mackey's posse disembarked and began what would be the first of many raids. The raiders swarmed over gambling houses and left smashed-up, burned-out shells in their wake. Mackey's repeated raids combined with a 100 percent conviction rate of arrestees ensured him victory over Northern Virginia's casino town and guaranteed him three terms in office as Attorney General.

Today, few reminders of this period in history remain. There is no trace of Jackson City today, the land area is now occupied by the Pentagon, Crystal City and the Del Ray neighborhood. In 2014, a park that had been named in Mackey's honor was replaced by new developments.

At the tail end of Jackson City's heyday, one of the most colorful men Washington had ever seen set up his own gambling shop at the "Monte Carlo of the Potomac." The legendary career of "Gentleman Gambler," Jimmy La Fontaine spanned half a century, from the end of the 19th century to the beginning of the 20th. The last of the gas-light era gamblers was one of Joe Nesline's earliest mentors and friend.

6

"The Noble Experiment"

Prohibition

Even before the Mafia had organized the entire American underworld, it had strong communication lines into Washington. These were first built-up during the Prohibition Era, when gangsters passed money back to the capital for their own protection. During the lawless days of Prohibition, the underworld began the process of undermining the honesty of local, state and even federal officials.

Up until the 18th Amendment to the U.S. Constitution in 1919, which established the prohibition of intoxicating liquors in the United States, lawbreakers feared

"Uncle Sam". There were few federal criminal laws and most criminals didn't want to tangle with the Feds. Only unsophisticated amateurs got involved with the Postal Inspectors or the Secret Service.

The National Prohibition Act, also known as the Volstead Act, was enacted to carry out the intent of the 18th Amendment. The Anti-Saloon League conceived and drafted the bill, which was named for Congressman Andrew Volstead of Minnesota, the Chairman of the House Judiciary Committee who managed the legislation. With the start of the Prohibition Era and the wholesale bribery and corruption of the 1920s, respect for federal law enforcement plummeted.

According to Howard Abadinsky, Criminal Justice Professor at St. John's University in New York City, the term "organized crime" didn't really exist in the United States before Prohibition. Criminal gangs had run amok in American cities since the late 19th century, but they were mostly bands of street thugs running small-time extortion and loan-sharking rackets in predominantly ethnic neighborhoods.

In fact, before the passing of the 18th Amendment, it wasn't mobsters who ran the most organized criminal schemes in America, but corrupt political "Bosses." Powerful political machines employed gangs as thugs. "They intimidated opposition and funneled votes to the boss. In return, the politicians and police chiefs turned a blind eye to illegal gambling and prostitution rings." But the under-world power dynamics shifted dramatically with the onset of Prohibition. With the overnight outlawing of alcohol in America legitimate distillers, brewers and saloons were put out of business. The mobsters stepped in to quench the powerful thirst of the "Roaring Twenties."

The key to running a successful bootlegging operation was a paramilitary organization. At first, the street gangs didn't know a thing about business, but they knew how to handle a gun and how to intimidate the competition. They could protect their rum-running operations from rival gangs, provide security for speakeasies and pay off cops and politicians.

It wasn't long before the mobsters were raking in millions and it was the political bosses and cops who were taking the orders. As the money kept pouring in, these formerly small-time street thugs got street-smart. They hired lawyers and accountants to launder the ill-gotten cash that was piling up. They started thinking strategically, investing in real estate, partnering with other gangs across ethnic lines and creating the logistics for shipping their product, both interstate and international. They had to become businessmen, and that gave rise to "Syndicated Crime" or what is now called organized crime. Before Prohibition, criminal gangs were local menaces, but the overwhelming business opportunity of illegal booze changed everything and Prohibition was the major catalyst.

The "Noble Experiment" of Prohibition began nationwide in 1920, but Washington, D.C. went dry on November 1, 1917. Congress intended the nation's capital to be the model dry city for the country. Prior to Prohibition, the city of Washington was relatively quiet. The seat of the American government did not really start to swing until booze became taboo. After Prohibition the embassies which are legally classified as foreign soil were suddenly given an unprecedented social advantage. Drinks could be served all day and night if the diplomats were so inclined. The format of having parties and getting business accomplished through these soirees became well established and continued even after Prohibition was repealed.

As a result of the wanton disregard for the law of the land, the Washington metropolitan area ended up with more than 3,000 speakeasies. It has been estimated that bootleggers transported 22,000 gallons of liquor a week to supply the city's saloons, social clubs and speakeasies. U.S. Navy personnel brought rum from Cuba to the Navy Yard in Southeast Washington, D.C. Congress even had its own private bootlegger, George L. Cassiday Sr., better known as "The Man in the Green Hat," who secretly delivered booze to the majority of Congress for ten years. The five presidents who served during the Prohibition Era were known to raise an occasional cocktail glass in defiance of the law. This illegal activity spilled over on to the streets of the capitol, where car chases between the rum runners and the police defined the social scene in the District. Joe Nesline crashed a high-powered touring car full of booze in a high-speed chase with the police on one of his liquor runs. In 1930, during the later years of Prohibition, 17-year-old Joe Nesline did a three-year prison stretch for bootlegging.

The 21st Amendment to the United States Constitution repealed the 18th Amendment. The 21st Amendment was ratified by Congress on December 5,

1933. It is unique among the 27 amendments to the Constitution for being the only one to repeal a prior amendment, as well as being the only amendment to have been ratified by state ratifying conventions.

Today, tourists to D.C. can still find traces of this illicit past. Most of the notable locations of this tumultuous time were destroyed. Many speakeasies were renovated or torn down, but a few key sites survive. One of the sites is the Historic Gaslight Building, located at 1020 16th Street N.W., formerly the residence of Ulysses S. Grant. The speakeasy was known as the Gaslight Club which was hidden on the third floor. The secret entrance was located in the men's room and could only be entered when the patron turned a faucet handle, which opened a hidden door. The original three-story building still exists with renovations and the addition of five extra stories.

Another speakeasy was the Tune Inn, located on 331 Pennsylvania Avenue S.E., in the shadow of the Capitol Dome. During Prohibition, the Tune Inn appeared to be a simple candy shop. However, if the patrons knew the right word, they would have been allowed to descend to the basement where alcohol could be purchased. These days the Tune Inn is a legal watering hole frequented by Congresspersons as well as local cops and federal agents. The proprietors of the Tune Inn claim the establishment obtained the second legal liquor license issued by the city.

The swankiest D.C. speakeasy and gambling spot was the Mayflower Club located on the fourth floor of 1223 Connecticut Avenue N.W. According to Garrett Peck, the author of "Prohibition In Washington, D.C.: How Dry We Weren't," the speakeasy was home to a 30-foot bar that served elegant cocktails to high-society clients and was decorated with a mural of Mahatma Gandhi and other famous figures playing the piano. In 1933, in the waning days of Prohibition, police raided the speakeasy, seizing large quantities of illegal alcohol and arrested the proprietor, Zacharia "Zebbie" Goldsmith. When Prohibition was repealed just before the trial date, his attorney managed to get the charges dropped. Police finally nabbed "Zebbie" a year later for failure to pay liquor taxes and allowing gambling. If you want to visit the site of the old Mayflower Club, it is now known as Zebbie's Garden, an upscale nightclub and garden.

In the Ivy City section of Northeast, D.C. the Green Hat Distillery, which operated from 2012 to 2022, was the first distillery in Washington since before Prohibition. But that wasn't the company's only link to the city's teetotaling past. The distillery's signature product, "Green Hat Gin" was an homage to Congress' own personal bootlegger, George Cassiday "The Man in the Green Hat." The distillery has since moved its operation to Kansas, although their gin can be bought in a Capitol Hill liquor store located just blocks away from the 1920's action. The Ivy City neighborhood is known as "Distillery Row" of Washington, D.C.

7
"Muscling In on D.C. Rackets"
Jimmy LaFontaine
"The Gentleman Gambler"

James A. "Jimmy" La Fontaine
(photo Washington Post obituary)

In the early 20th century Washington, D.C. had its own gambling kingpin, Jimmy LaFontaine. After earning startup capital from his gambling operation on the District's southern border in the now defunct "Jackson City," Virginia, he moved to the District's northern border. In 1917, Jimmy began buying up property on the corner of Eastern Avenue and Bladensburg Road in Prince George's County, Maryland. By the time he was done, he had converted an aging ornate mansion into a rough but ready casino known as the Maryland Athletic Club, which enjoyed a bustling business. Mafia associated gamblers like Joseph Nesline and his Steubenville, Ohio pal Dino Cellini honed their skills working at Jimmy's Place.

Though Jimmy's operation inevitably brought unwelcome attention from mobsters and law enforcement, he is most often remembered as Washington's "Gentleman Gambler." He was known to refund the money of gamblers who couldn't afford the loss and ban them from future visits to the club. Losers who could afford a tough tap were treated to a free meal and a ride home.

From the 1920s to the 1940s, the Maryland Athletic Club, commonly known as Jimmy's Place, was the place to gamble in the Washington area and beyond. At its height, it was the largest casino between Saratoga, New York and Palm Beach, Florida. The club was regularly frequented by some of Washington's biggest movers and shakers, including the FBI's J. Edgar Hoover.

The key to La Fontaine's success lay in lessons he learned years earlier when he operated his short-lived establishment in Jackson City. While there, Jimmy observed that many people who opposed gambling did not take issue with gambling per se, instead they took issue with the criminal activities which were often associated with gambling. So, if he could keep criminal elements, besides the illegal gambling itself, away from his casino, then it was less likely to be a target for the police.

With that in mind, Jimmy's casino had a few very strict rules:

- Alcohol was banned and every single patron was frisked for flasks before entry.

- Guns were not permitted. Remarkably, FBI Director J. Edgar Hoover and his men once kicked up a fuss when they were asked to surrender their pistols but Jimmy held his ground. Desperate to gamble in a place some might have demanded they raid, the G-men gave in.
- Finally, Jimmy's Place also banned women. According to an 1891 report by the D.C. Police; "lewd women, using vile and filthy language, frequented Jackson City and presented a disgusting spectacle."

While others may have scoffed, La Fontaine's policies turned out to be very good for business. So, it seems Jimmy's Place was an anomaly, a casino with no wine, women or weapons. The establishment also served food, but with a limited menu. You could order anything you wanted as long as it was beef stew, which was said to be "pretty good." Jimmy's Place became a cash cow. His gambling enterprise was so profitable he himself admitted to paying thousands of dollars a year to informants who warned him of upcoming raids, and in bribes to local officials for protection. Geography afforded Jimmy's Place certain advantages. The casino's driveway was in D.C., while the building sat in Maryland. This proved quite convenient on occasions when police investigated the club after receiving complaints. When raided the patrons simply fled a few yards into the other jurisdiction. Similarly, police in both jurisdictions, a number of whom were also patrons of Jimmy's Place themselves, were known to claim it lay outside of their jurisdiction. The house limit was $10 on numbers, $200 on craps, $500 on blackjack, and had no-limit games in private rooms for certain high-rollers. La Fontaine also made horse book. "Jimmy's" Place catered to as many as 2,000 gamblers a night.

Charlie Ford, a Washington lawyer and counsel for gamblers, vice hucksters, and bottle-clubs was the trustee of La Fontaine's estate. In this capacity some complicated book-keeping was required. With the questionable accounting, Jimmy served a jail term for income-tax evasion and paid a fine of $200,000. La Fontaine also controlled the entire underworld in the Maryland counties adjoining the District. All this ensured the illegal casino's longevity and contributed to Jimmy's legend. However, all eras must eventually come to an end. In 1939, the Boo Boo Hoff Mob muscled in on Jimmy's Place. While they kept Jimmy as the face of the operation, the gang took the profits. The Bladensburg Road casino saw bets for another eight years before closing in 1947. Jimmy La Fontaine passed away two years later and upon his death eighty percent of his assets went to the Syndicate.

Jimmy LaFontaine died of a cerebral hemorrhage in 1949. Newspapers throughout the Washington-Baltimore area published long obituaries honoring Jimmy but despite his legendary status, Jimmy's memory faded fast. On February 5, 1955, firefighters torched Jimmy's Place to clear the land for the construction of a Giant Food Stores distribution center.

Today, the site is occupied by warehouses. Few passersby would have any idea that the spot was once home to an institution of D.C. nightlife and the pride of the Gentleman Gambler.

The following is a summary from an October 11, 1976, Sports Illustrated article written by Charles Price, the son of Jimmy La Fontaine's casino manager:

After the Prohibition Era, Mr. Jim (La Fontaine) had been kidnapped by some out-of-town racketeers for $40,000 ransom. Three men spirited him, blindfolded, to a backwoods cottage in Virginia. There they waited for three days, but nobody offered to pay Mr. Jim's ransom. That bothered Mr. Jim not at all. To kill time, he suggested that they play some hearts. Mr. Jim beat them out of several thousand dollars for which he took a marker. On the fifth day the kidnappers began getting nervous. Finally, one of the men blew his stack, "Why doesn't somebody pay your ransom?" he demanded. "That's easy," said Mr. Jim. "I'm the only guy I know who's got $40,000, and nobody knows where I keep my money. But I'll tell you what. You take me home, and I'll get your money for you." They drove Mr. Jim to his row house. True to his word, Mr. Jim strolled into the house, kissed Miss Annie on the cheek as though he had been away on a business trip, then walked back to the car with 40 one thousand-dollar bills. He counted out 36 of them and tucked the other four back in his pocket. "These are what you owe me for the hearts game," he said and walked away.

8

"Philadelphia Incursion"

The "Boo Boo" Hoff Mob

Gangster Max "Boo Boo" Hoff

With four fighters that he managed ca. 1930s

(photo Temple University Libraries)

The syndicate had long cast covetous eyes on Jimmy's Casino. The legendary Gentleman Gambler's era eventually came to an end in 1939, when the "Boo Boo" Hoff Mob of Philadelphia muscled in on Jimmy's Place. Following Jimmy's kidnapping and the ransom he self-paid, the Mob declared themselves in on his enterprise.

While the Mob kept Jimmy on as the face of the operation, the gang took the profits. Eighty percent of his holdings belonged to the Syndicate. Jimmy's pay-off to the top was made through Harry ("Nig" Rosen") Stromberg of Philadelphia to Meyer Lansky of New York. Lansky answered to Frank Costello and his gambling partner Joe Adonis. The same scenario of taking over local rackets and turning them into subsidiaries of the Syndicate happened in every major American city. By the 1930s the Mob was dominant in every racket. The only way local operators could do business was to accept the over-lordship of the Mob. If they cooperated, they were allowed to continue and prosper.

Max "Boo Boo" Hoff was born in South Philadelphia. Hoff was an ex-boxer who later became a bootlegger and gambler. In 1929 Hoff, along with "Nig Rosen" attended the Atlantic City, New Jersey Conference. The meeting took place at the Ritz-Carlton and Ambassador Hotels on the Boardwalk. The conference coincided with Jewish Mob boss Meyer Lansky's wedding in Atlantic City.

At the conference, the men discussed the future structure of organized crime and the Mafia in America. From May 13th to 16th, 1929, Atlantic County Treasurer and political boss Enoch Lewis "Nucky" Johnson hosted the Atlantic City Conference. Johnson made arrangements for the attendees' accommodations and guaranteed there would be no law enforcement interference since his brother, Alfred Johnson, was the Sheriff of Atlantic County. The conference was called by "Lucky" Luciano from New York and Johnny Torrio from Chicago. Also from Chicago were Al Capone and Jake "Greasy Thumb" Guzik. Other attendees from New York and New Jersey included: Meyer Lansky, "Bugsy" Siegel, Frank Costello, Joe Adonis, Carlo Gambino, Gaetano Lucchese, Albert Anastasia, Louis "Lepke" Buchalter, Abner Zwillman, Dutch Schultz and others. Abe Bernstein represented Detroit's "Purple Gang." The Kansas City and Cleveland factions were represented. Max "Boo Boo" Hoff and Harry "Nig" Rosen represented Philadelphia.

In the 2010 to 2014, HBO series "Boardwalk Empire," Steve Buscemi portrayed a character named Enoch "Nucky" Thompson. Shea Whigham portrayed Elias "Eli" Thompson, "Nucky's" brother and Atlantic County Sheriff.

9

"Neutral City"

Sit Down at the Shoreham Hotel

The Mob has never been as strong in D.C. as it has been in other American cities. There have been several attempts to explain this. One is that D.C. was too small a town to bother with. Then there are unconfirmed reports that J. Edgar Hoover struck some sort of deal with Frank Costello to keep the Mob out. It has also been rumored that Meyer Lansky was in possession of compromising photographs of Mr. Hoover, however, none have ever surfaced. An investigative reporter and author who moved to Washington, D.C. tells a different story. After learning of a mob contract on his life in the 1970s, federal agents had suggested to the reporter that he move to a neutral town, one in which the Mafia factions shared turf, with none of them dominant. The reporter chose Washington, D.C.

Before the underworld was completely organized, Washington was a "neutral" city, where mob meetings and conventions were held. In such cities the delegates must not pack guns or engage in any rough stuff. Other such cities were Saratoga Springs, New York, Hot Springs, Arkansas, Las Vegas, Nevada, Atlantic City, New Jersey and Miami, Florida. These were important resort centers, and were kept neutral because any acts of extreme gun-play might scare away paying customers. In those days they knew that ride-by shootings would not be tolerated in the nation's Capital, at least not until the 1980s and 1990s.

William Garber, an attorney who represented local crime figures, told a Washington Post reporter in the 1980s that "organized crime thought moving into Washington would just be pushing the FBI too far." William Garber was a defense attorney who started his practice in Washington, D.C. in the 1950s. He clerked for Charlie Ford, an old-time "Fifth Street" lawyer. In the 1950s, Bill Garber and Charlie Ford's criminal clientele were largely gamblers, bootleggers, robbers and drug dealers.

One of the best reasons why the Mafia did not have direct control on criminal enterprises in the District comes from the 1951 book "Washington Confidential" by Jack Lait and Lee Mortimer. "A city administration can be bought or scared or rigged. But nobody can capture 96 Senators and 435 Representatives. Anyone of these at the time was the immediate boss of Washington and anyone of them could have arisen any day and demanded a probe." This was before Alaska and Hawaii entered the Union and before Home Rule for the District of Columbia.

Before the Racketeer Influenced Corrupt Organization (RICO) laws were enacted in 1970, the FBI's jurisdiction was circumscribed by Congress, and the mobsters were smart enough to keep out of fields in which the FBI may act. Hoover much preferred going after bank robbers, kidnappers, anarchists and especially communists. Another reason for Director Hoover's reluctance to have his Bureau involved in Mob investigations may have been his gambling habit, especially betting on the horses. It has been theorized that Hoover pocketed his winnings but his losses were covered by New York Boss Frank Costello. Before the FBI became actively involved the two main federal agencies that investigated and gathered intelligence on the Mob was the U.S. Secret Service and the Bureau of Narcotics, two agencies which fell under the Department of the Treasury.

In the 1930s, Chicago Outfit hitman, "Machine Gun" Jack McGurn (Vincenzo Antonio Gibaldi) was summoned from Chicago to the neutral city of Washington, D.C. for a meeting of his peers. New York Commission Boss Charlie "Lucky" Luciano had called for a week-long set of meetings at the Blue Room of the Shoreham Hotel on Calvert Street N.W. McGurn had been getting out of line and was on trial for his life. The attendees, all under assumed names, included Frank Nitti (Chicago), Izzie Bernstein (Purple Gang, Detroit), and other hoods. Jack McGurn was eventually assassinated in 1936.

Harry J. Anslinger, the Commissioner of the Treasury's Bureau of Narcotics and the "Father of the War on Drugs", interrupted the gangster convention after catching wind of the Mob meeting, he had "Lucky" called out to the hotel lobby. Luciano was offended, and complained about the interruption of his party, saying, "You can't do anything to me. We got Constitutional rights, we're only sight-seeing." Anslinger noted the bejeweled female escorts of the attendees and retorted, "That's all you'd better do. Remember the Mann Act." The Mann Act (White-Slave Traffic Act) was a United States federal law, passed June 25, 1910. The law was named after Congressman James Robert Mann of Illinois. The

Act made it a felony to engage in interstate or foreign commerce or transport of any woman or girl for the purpose of prostitution.

Harry Jacob Anslinger
1st Commissioner of the Federal Bureau of Narcotics
(photo DEA Museum)

In the 1950s Commissioner Anslinger formed his own "Italian Squad," a group of Italian-American narcotics agents specifically tasked to investigate the "French Connection," the Corsican Mafia's heroin trade between France, Canada and the United States. The squad was headed by Agent Charles Siragusa who helped convict "Lucky" Luciano in 1936. Siragusa continued to investigate Luciano even after the Mob Boss' deportation to Italy.

The original "Italian Squad" was formed in the early 1900s by the New York City Police Department (NYPD). It was a team of Italian American police officers who spoke the varied regional dialects of the Italian language. They were tasked with investigating the "Black Hand" extortionists preying on the Italian immigrant enclaves. The squad was headed by Italian born Detective Lieutenant Joseph Petrosino. The NYPD detective traveled to Italy on a secret mission to obtain court records. He reasoned that in order to stop the flow of criminals from Italy, it was necessary to refuse entry to those immigrants with prison records. Petrosino's mission was leaked and he was assassinated in Sicily on March 12, 1909. The NYPD's "Italian Squad" eventually became the Bomb Squad and Canine Unit, the first units of their kind in the United States.

In the 1950 movie "Black Hand" starring Gene Kelley, Lieutenant Joseph Petrosino is portrayed by J. Carrol Naish. In the 1960 BioPic "Pay or Die," Petrosino is portrayed by Ernest Borgnine. A plaque dedicated to the police officer is located in Lieutenant (Giuseppe) Petrosino Square in a city park in the Little Italy section of Manhattan.

10

"Self Defense"

A Killing at the Hide-Away Club

George "Mad Dog" Harding

Lone-Wolf gun for hire killed by Joe Nesline

(photo Washington Evening Star)

In the early morning hours of January 10, 1951, Joe Nesline shot and killed another mobster named George Paul Harding. The shooting took place in the second-floor staircase of the Hide-Away club which was located in the District's Georgetown waterfront area at 3135 K Street N.W. The building beneath what is now the Whitehurst Freeway, was originally a barrel factory in the late 1800s. It was home to various clubs starting in the 1930s, including the after-hours joint the Hide-Away. The club was one of at least 500 after-hours "Bottle Clubs" operating in the city at the time. It is currently an AMC movie-plex.

George "Mad Dog" Harding, was known as a "lone-wolf," willing to hire out his gun and reputation to anyone who would pay. It had been quite a night for Harding that January in 1951. Earlier, he shot at a bartender and roughed up waitresses at clubs in the Maryland suburb of Prince George 's County.

At one of these, the Club Chesapeake in Cottage City, he'd spoken briefly to Nesline. The encounter was not friendly. The two childhood friends, who were from the same Northeast D.C. neighborhood, had had a "falling out" the previous year. One rumor at the time was that Harding, while drunk, had disrespected Nesline's first wife at their home.

By the time Harding got to the Hide-Away with convicted "White Slaver" George "The Greek" Clainos a little before 4am, Nesline had been there drinking for two hours. The two again had words.

At Nesline's murder trial, a waitress at the club, Juanita Gilbert, testified she witnessed "the Greek" handing over a gun to Harding who slipped it in his pocket. Gilbert also saw Harding become sick in the kitchen of the club, apparently having hit the bottle a little too hard. When he recovered, he showed her the gun and said "I'm going to take care of Nesline now." Juanita did not warn Nesline stating

"I don't like to get mixed up in that kind of thing. I'm a little afraid of guns and particularly of George Harding, especially with a gun."

Another waitress at the club, Harriet Harding, (no relation to "Mad Dog,") testified "He (Harding) had been drinking. Most every time I would see him, he had been drinking." On several occasions George Harding told her, "Collect my check from Nesline,... because he has the money." Harriet saw Nesline get up and start toward the stairway. Harding told the waitress, "Don't block my view." Harding then lunged at the waitress, knocking a tray out of her hands with a shout of "Get out of my way, baby" and bounded up the stairs to the balcony.

Two D.C. police officers, Lt. Karl McCormick and Sgt. Arthur Gernhofer had entered the club and heard the gunfire. They rushed to the stairway and saw Nesline coming down the stairs. Nesline told the officers, "I had to do it, he forced me into it. It was either Harding or me." Harding's body was found on the balcony floor outside the men's room. When the police rolled him over, powder burns on his chest showed he'd been shot at point-blank range. A loaded .38 caliber revolver fell from his right hip pocket.

For his murder trial, Joe Nesline retained the well-known D.C. criminal defense attorney Charles E. Ford. While on the stand Nesline testified; "He (Harding) was coming toward me, a step or two. He called me an awful name, and a stool pigeon, and said 'I don't want your money, I want your.....' He had taken his hands out of his pockets and was grabbing his coat. He had his coat open, as if he were

61

reaching for something. I believed he was going to shoot me, to kill me. I had this pistol between my pants and my shirt, and I reached out and pulled the trigger. The gun went off."

While on the stand testifying in his own defense, Nesline described himself as a secretary of the Wash-Tex Oil Co. The head of the corporation was Nesline's defense attorney Charlie Ford.

During the initial investigative phase of the Harding murder, Nesline told the police Harding had accused him of running out with Harding's share of the "gravy" in an oil deal in Texas. According to the authors of the book 'Washington Confidential" the man behind the Texas oil corporation was New York Mob Boss Frank Costello, who was buying leases and collecting royalties.

During the trial it was revealed that Nesline had gotten the gun from Anthony Celani. Celani was described as a car salesman in Alexandria, Virginia, and a poolroom operator in Northeast D.C. who also ran a limousine service. Nesline said he was carrying the gun because he was afraid. He knew sooner or later he would meet up with Harding again.

In his summation to the jury, Nesline's defense attorney Charlie Ford stated "When you're full of fear someone's going to kill you, you can't think straight. Nesline had no choice on that balcony in the Hide-Away Club at that moment except to defend himself. By the law of God it is the law that you have a right to defend yourself. Call him a gambler, call him what you will, but he still is entitled to the laws of God, of nature and of the District of Columbia." The jury believed him. Joe was acquitted of the murder but convicted of carrying an unlicensed .45 caliber pistol.

Washington Post reporter Benjamin Bradlee pointed out that the Judge in the case, Alexander Holtzoff was not happy with the verdict. The judge took the unusual step of questioning the jury's wisdom. "This defendant is a dangerous individual. He is a racketeer and professional gambler," Holtzoff declared. He wanted Joe convicted of manslaughter.

Joe received the maximum sentence of one year in jail for unlicensed weapons possession and a $1,000 fine. Twenty years later Ben Bradlee would go on to be the editor of the Washington Post during the Watergate scandal.

In her book "Lucky '325,'" Joe's wife, Josephine Alvarez believed the shooting had to do with Joe's old friend and mentor Emmett "Little Man" Warring, the former bootlegger and numbers racketeer. Local D.C. newspaper articles at the time agreed with that speculation. Nesline believed Harding set up a January 9, 1950 home invasion at Warring's Foggy Bottom home.

Three gunmen posing as deliverymen robbed Warring at his home located at 3900 Macomb Street, N.W. and made off with cash from Warring's pocket and from his safe. Josephine estimated that Warring's losses amounted to

$100,000 including his trademark diamond ring. Word on the street was that Harding, a former Warring bodyguard who was fired for beating up a girlfriend and thus gaining unwanted notoriety, had "put the finger" on his old boss.

The Italian born Harding (true name unknown) had a long and bloody career as a gunman, killer and "finger-man." In the vernacular of the underworld, a finger-man is a racketeer who surveys the scene of a potential crime, gathers necessary information and passes it on to the actual perpetrators in return for a share of the loot.

In 1933, Harding was convicted of manslaughter of a well-known gambler, Harry "Doc" Davis. "Doc" was the brother of D.C. Police Inspector O.T. Davis. Harding was paroled in 1937. Later, Harding was granted a full pardon under blanket amnesty for G.I.s who served in WWII by President Truman. During the war George "Mad Dog" Harding was a Sergeant in the U.S. Army Air Corp.

During the course of the police investigation of Warring's home invasion and robbery case, suspects were developed. The main suspect was Sidney Stromberg of Pottsville, Pennsylvania. Police discovered that Stromberg was registered in D.C.'s Ambassador Hotel between the 5th and the 9th of January 1950, under the assumed name of Sidney Max.

In September of 1951, three men were indicted and went to trial, but only Stromberg was convicted. A handwriting expert testified that the signature of

Sidney Max on the hotel registration matched the handwriting of Stromberg. During the trial Stromberg denied any collusion with Harding.

Several months before the Hide-Away shooting in November of 1950, George Harding had traveled to Pottsville, Pennsylvania and visited Stromberg who was pending trial on a manslaughter charge for killing a gambling house doorman. Stromberg was later convicted and sentenced to 6 to 12 years. Sidney was the younger brother of the previously mentioned Philadelphia mobster Harry ("Nig" Rosen) Stromberg.

Joe Nesline was very close to Emmitt Warring. Joe had gotten his start in the underworld running hooch for the Warring family operation. When Emmitt Warring died in 1974, Joe was the beneficiary in his Will. The assets Joe received were mostly his own, Nesline never had any credit cards, savings or checking accounts. Everything was cash and carry.

11

"Messaggero"

Gaetano Ricci

Gaetano "Big Tony" Ricci aka Anthony Goebbels

The most well-connected Mobster few have ever heard of

The man who brought Al Capone to Chicago

(photo Miami Herald)

The killing of George "Mad Dog" Harding by Joe Nesline was probably ordered from Mob headquarters in New York. The Mob saw Harding as an intemperate drinker who knew too much and talked too much. Several months earlier Harding was warned "to be good or else." The warning from New York was transmitted by Tony Ricci, who was the message-center for the Mob. New York's Genovese Family is credited with inventing the position of "Messaggero." The job of the messenger is to function as liaison between specific families. The messenger

66

reduced the need for sit-downs and limited the exposure of bosses to law enforcement. The position was originally set up to coordinate activities with the New York Mob's counterpart in Chicago.

Gaetano "Big Tony" Ricci aka Anthony Goebbels was the Genovese family's "Messagerro" between New York and Mafia Families of the Mid-West. "Big Tony" was born in Italy in 1893, he emigrated with his family to Brooklyn, New York when he was 5 years old. He was naturalized a U.S. citizen in 1944.

After retiring his position as a Capo in the Genovese crime family, he became the chief coordinator of Mafia activities between New York and Chicago and a traveling courier; delivering orders, messages and news around the country. In November 1952, U.S. Attorney General James P. McGranery ordered denaturalization proceedings in Brooklyn against New York underworld figures. In the petition Ricci was described as a former partner of Charles "Lucky" Luciano and a close associate of racketeers on the East coast and the Mid-West. The petition accused Ricci of making fraudulent representations as to his place of residence and as to his activities. It was one of many proceedings in the Attorney General's program for ridding the country of some 100 persons he regarded as undesirable.

Ricci was also one of hundreds of witnesses called to testify before the "Kefauver Committee,' officially known as the Special Committee on Organized Crime in Interstate Commerce. During the course of the 15-month investigation, the committee met in 14 major U.S. cities and interviewed hundreds of witnesses in open televised executive session. The committee dissolved on September 1, 1951.

12

"Shocked, shocked to find that gambling is going on in here!"

A Congressional Committee

In 1951, due in part to the killing of George Harding by Joe Nesline, an article appeared in the Washington Post which stated; "Behind it's glittering social life and pompous governmental operations, the nation's capital now stands revealed as a city in which thrives criminal activity of shocking enormity." That was the finding of a congressional committee studying lawlessness and vice in the District of Columbia. "Big shot gamblers well known to the public and friendly to the police, enjoyed a charmed existence. The city is infested with after-hours clubs, which exist under special law originally designed to permit the organization of charitable and humanitarian groups. The sole purpose of these clubs now is to provide a place for the sale of liquor after normal tavern closing hours. These clubs breed crime, afford prostitutes and panderers a convenient base of operation and give criminals the means of playing host to those who patronize them."

The murder, which rocked the Washington underworld and the establishment alike, heightened the outcry from congress and newspapers demanding action on after-hours clubs. The Hide-Away Club was permanently shut down by the owner of the property, auto dealer Percy Klein. A congressional committee formed to investigate the problem in the District had recommended legislation to shut down clubs such as the Hide-Away only a week before the murder. Supposedly, these clubs were private benevolent organizations which operated after regular bars were by law shut for the night. The "Bottle Clubs" served 40-cent set-ups for members who kept their own booze on the premises. The Congressional Committee described them as private gambling dens and all-night speakeasies that openly flouted D.C. liquor laws.

The congressional committee focused most of its attention on gambling. It found that there were bookies and numbers racket agents operating brazenly in almost every government facility including the buildings which housed the offices of the U.S. Bureau of Prisons and even the Kefauver Committee, which at the time was investigating organized crime in America.

Superintendent of the D.C. Police Department Robert J. Barrett also became a focal point of the commission's wide-ranging investigation into gambling kickbacks and narcotics dealings. In 1947, then Captain Barrett, the close friend of Philadelphia mobster Harry "Nig" Rosen, was the lowest ranking police official to be promoted to Major Superintendent (Chief of Police) of the D.C. Metropolitan Police Department. Complaining of ill health, Barrett retired from the department and neglected to appear before the commission. When he finally

sat before the commission, he refused to answer any questions. In 1957, Barrett
was indicted for tax evasion.

To quote British actor Claude Rains as Captain Renault,
in the casino scene from the classic 1942 movie "Casablanca,"
the Kefauver Committee was;
"Shocked, shocked to find that gambling is going on in here!"

13

"Fifth Street Cicero"

Charles E. Ford

The Superior Court of the District of Columbia is at the southern terminus of Fifth Street, N.W. The neighborhood is known as Judiciary Square and is located between Pennsylvania Avenue to the south, H Street to the north, 6th Street to the west, and the access tunnel to I 395 to the east. It is mostly occupied by various federal and municipal courthouses and office buildings including the U.S Attorney's office. The center of the neighborhood is an actual plaza named Judiciary Square which is between D.C.'s Metropolitan Police Headquarters and the D.C. Superior Court.

"Fifth Street" used to be home to some of the best trial lawyers in D.C.'s history. It had been the heart of the District's legal world since the 19th century, and by the 1930s telling someone, "Go down to Fifth Street and get yourself a good lawyer" was a gentle way of saying, "You've got a problem." Charles E. Ford, was known as the "Fifth Street Cicero" (Cicero was ancient Rome's greatest lawyer, statesman and orator). Ford was a flamboyant advocate for his clients. While assigned to the municipal courts, a young Washington Post reporter wrote, "The biggest gamblers in the District were represented by a colorful lawyer named Charlie Ford, the self-proclaimed president of the 'Fifth Street Bar Association.'

Ford was masterful with juries; corny, scornful, humble, tricky, laughing, tear–stained you name it. He had a Robin Hood fee schedule, a pittance for poor people charged with serious crimes, ten times as much for the rich no matter how minor the offence. He once dispatched a client's first-degree murder charge by dramatically accusing him of manslaughter."

Ford started practicing law during the Prohibition Era in the early 1920's. He was the darling of gambling and prostitution society. The police didn't feel so bad when they lost to Ford since he was a great friend to the cops, and represented the Policeman's Benevolent Society free of charge. Ford was Joe Nesline's lawyer as well as Emmitt "Little Man" Warring, Joe's friend and mentor, the bootlegger and numbers operator. Ford was also the trustee of "Gentleman Gambler" Jimmy La Fontaine's estate after his death.

Very few of Ford's clients spent time in jail after arrest. When a defendant, usually a numbers runner or a prostitute, was booked at the police station, they put in a phone call to a designated number. Then one of a number of bail-bondsmen would get a call, and within a short time the bondsman appeared at the police station and put-up surety for the arrestee. One of the bailers utilized by the organization that backed Ford's clients was Meyer Weinstein who was still operating into the 1980s. The arrestees seldom paid their bail-bond fee or knew who contacted the bondsman or who paid the fee.

Charlie Ford appeared in Chicago and successfully convinced the Kefauver committee it couldn't force Anna Fischetti to testify against her husband, Charles Fischetti, the notorious Capone gangster. He successfully defied the Congressional committee which tried to make him divulge the names of his clients, though he admitted Emmitt Warring was one. The others, Ford said were known to the public only as respectable businessmen. They were "more powerful" than Warring or even Jimmy La Fontaine, who were only "peanut-peddlers compared to them." None of Charlie's law firm clients ever got the electric chair. One was sentenced to death for murder, but saved the firm's record by considerately hanging himself in jail.

Charlie was a large, flamboyant guy who loved to socialize and loved to eat. He was very popular, especially with newspapermen. He fed them plenty of liquor and also plenty of background material on gangsters and criminals without violating his legal ethics. Charlie also operated two celebrated restaurants which were left to him in a will when the restaurateur passed away. Charlie patronized and entertained at these restaurants freely. Whenever he needed a respite from his overindulgence, he would go to Hot Springs, Arkansas, for the reducing baths and a few days of relaxation with his friend Owney "The Killer" Madden. Owen Vincent "Owney" Madden was the English born retired Gang Chieftain from Manhattan who operated the famous "Cotton Club" in Harlem, New York City.

14

"Legend of the Line"

Bob Martin

Robert "Bob Martin" Blume

(photo wiseguys. Com)

From 1967 to 1983, the world of sports betting revolved around the "Las Vegas Line." You could make a bet in any city in America, but the point spread you had to beat originated in Las Vegas, in the mind of one man; Robert "Bob Martin" Blume. Martin was a friend and associate of Joe Nesline and was regarded as the greatest oddsmaker in the history of sport. Operating in New York City, he made out all right until the 1951 college basketball point-shaving scandals, when he was wiped out by those in on the fixes.

Born in 1918, in Brooklyn, Martin loved talking baseball with the customers at his parent's delicatessen. He put his sports knowledge to use by betting quarters at neighborhood poolrooms. As a teenager he began taking some sports betting action himself from other high school kids. Martin continued taking bets in France while assigned to an anti-aircraft battery in World War II. He came out of the Army with $30,000. With that kind of money, Martin figured he could make a living betting on baseball, basketball and football and later on boxing. But it was the insiders involved in the 1950-1951 point-shaving basketball scandals that broke him. Teams started throwing games and he could not overcome the fix. The scandal involved the National Invitation Tournament (NIT), the National Collegiate Athletic Association (NCAA) and the champion City College of New York (CCNY).

In 1952, "Crippled" Julius Silverman, a Washington, D.C. bookie, hired Martin to advise him on fighters. Martin made his living in D.C., working out of a building near the old State Department, operating there until 1959 when Martin, Silverman and Meyer "Nutsy" Schwartz were arrested in a Foggy Bottom row house. Their organization had become the number one boxing book in the country when Martin and his two partners were arrested.

Court records show that in the spring of 1958, the Washington D.C. Metropolitan Police and Agents of the Internal Revenue Service (IRS) had reason to suspect that the premises at 408 21st Street, N.W., was being used as the headquarters of a gambling operation. For three days in April 1958, the officers employed a so-called "spike mike" to listen to what was going on within the four walls of the house next door. The "spike mike" was a microphone with a spike about a foot long attached to it, together with an amplifier, a power pack and earphones. The officers inserted the spike under a baseboard in a room of the vacant house and into a crevice extending several inches into the party wall, until the spike hit something solid that acted as a sounding board. The spike made contact with a heating duct serving the house, thus converting their entire heating system into a conductor of sound. Conversations taking place in the house were audible to the officers through the earphones, and their testimony regarding these conversations which was admitted at the trial played a substantial part in the defendant's convictions.

When the three were arrested, they retained Edward Bennett Williams to represent them. The famed Washington, D.C. restauranteur and gambler, Duke Ziebert helped Bob Martin with his legal fees. Over lunch at Duke's restaurant, Williams predicted that the defendants would be convicted and their convictions affirmed by the D.C. Circuit but that the Supreme Court would unanimously reverse on fourth amendment grounds. Julius was disheartened and was convinced he would lose all the way to the Supreme Court. Joe Nesline was at the lunch table and told Julius he had confidence in Ed Williams and bet Julius he was going to win. Julius perked up and said "How much you wanna bet, Joe?" "Ten thousand says you win," Nesline said. "OK," Julius said. "You're on. But it has to be unanimous, like Williams said." Joe gave Duke the ten thousand to hold. Ed Williams made a $1000 side bet with Bob Martin that he would sweep the judges, 9-0 in the Silverman vs. United States landmark case. Martin, who was not as confident in attorney Williams as Nesline, bet him he wouldn't.

Sure enough, the defendants were convicted. The court of appeals affirmed the conviction and the Supreme Court granted certiorari (an order by which a higher court reviews a decision of a lower court). Ed Williams argued the case on December 5, 1960. Julius went to the Supreme Court every day and awaited the decision. Finally, on March 6, 1961, the Court decided the case. Julius went to the pay phone in the hall and called Duke Zeibert. "Duke, I won! I won!" "Oh great Julius," said Duke. "But was it unanimous? Joe will want to know." "Nope," said Julius. "Sorry. Two of them, well two of them said they concurred." The defendants escaped jail time after surveillance used to gather evidence was ruled illegal and a violation of the defendants' Fourth Amendment rights against unreasonable search and seizure. Martin was quite happy to pay Williams the $1,000. The record does not show if Julius Silverman paid off the bet to Joe Nesline.

Silverman's operation shut its doors in 1962 with Robert Kennedy's war on gambling in full swing. In 1963 Martin decided Washington was not big enough for both him and Attorney General Robert Kennedy. He relocated to Las Vegas, where bookmakers were legal. For a few years he made his living mostly as a bettor. In 1967 he was invited to manage the sports book at the new Churchill Downs betting parlor. He also spent three years working for the Union Plaza book in the mid-1970s, but it was at the Las Vegas' Churchill Downs betting parlor that his posted numbers first became the "Las Vegas Line" followed by bookmakers, legal and illegal, all over the country.

15

"Oldest Established Permanent Floating
Crap Game in D.C."

Cat and Mouse Game with the Feds

From the late 1950s to the mid 1960s, Joe Nesline and the Feds were engaged in a cat and mouse game over Joe's gambling operation in the Washington metropolitan area. In 1959 Joe opened a club in the District called the Spartan-American Club located at 1016-A 14th Street N.W. It did not take long for the club to be raided by the D.C. Police. Telephone wiretaps and phone records showed a high volume of calls from a sports betting operation in Norfolk, Virginia to a telephone in the Spartan-American Club. The U.S. Attorney's office believed the club was the Washington terminus of a major baseball betting syndicate. It appears Joe was expecting the raid and was waiting for the police when they arrived. The Assistant US Attorney assigned to the investigation was quoted in the Washington Evening Star newspaper; "Nesline was grinning like a Cheshire cat when police raiders arrived." The raid turned out to be a bust, no evidence of a sports betting operation was found. Thus began a campaign of law enforcement harassment, especially of the club's patrons. The continued police attention to Joe's Spartan-American club forced the establishment to close by December of 1961.

Joe then opened two new places in the District, the Amber Club and the Oriental-American Club. His new clubs were full-service gambling establishments with blackjack, craps and roulette. They were located in the Southeast section of Pennsylvania Avenue. The clubs were frequented by Senators, Congressmen, politicians, businessmen and local gamblers. Politically related events were always a busy time for the clubs. Joe's partners Charlie Tourine and Frank "Lefty" Rosenthal had an interest in the Amber Club. Another of Joe's associates, George Rohanna was the front-man for the Oriental-American Club. Rohanna had applied for a Certificate of Occupancy as a private club which attracted the attention of the authorities.

Law enforcement's harassment of the patrons continued at the new establishments. Joe lodged a legal protest and hired the law firm of Edward Bennett Williams to represent the clubs. In late 1962, Joe temporarily closed his clubs and went to Miami. In January of 1963, Joe had a reopening of the Spartan-American Club which was attended by a large crowd of patrons. The police pressure continued and the club closed for good in February of 1963. In a July 1963 FBI report, Nesline was reportedly overheard commenting that he attempted to re-open his dice game at the Amber Club, but was unable to do so because he could not obtain the necessary police protection. The captain of the precinct was cooperating, but somebody higher up was giving him a hard time.

He finally moved his gambling operation along with all the equipment and furniture to Maryland.

For the next five months Nesline and his associates, including Langhorne "Lang" Rorer and Gabriel "Gabby" Bobrow, would continue operating his floating craps games from La Plata, Maryland and Washington, D.C. down to Hampton, Virginia. To paraphrase a song from the 1950 Broadway musical "Guys and Dolls," Joe was running "the oldest established permanent floating craps game in D.C." This cat and mouse game continued until Nesline could open a permanent location in Maryland.

In June of 1963, Nesline opened The Sportsman Club in St. Mary's County, in southern Maryland. Joe and his partners estimated that if they could stay open for at least six months, they could make a million dollars. Joe along with Charlie Tourine renamed the new club "George Raft's Rendezvous." The plan was to have a restaurant modeled after Joe's friend Duke Zeibert's landmark dining establishment in D.C. Joe was a regular patron at Duke's restaurant. Present at the grand opening of the Club was the actor George Raft and singer Keely Smith, the wife of band leader Louie Prima.

The club was described as very plush and equipped with a lounge where one could buy drinks. Before entering the game room, one had to pass through three doors. The club held roulette, dice and blackjack tables. Bottles of Arpège perfume were handed out to the ladies as favors. Nesline himself worked as a dealer during the grand opening. Supposedly, Joe had obtained protection from local law enforcement and planned on operating for an indefinite period of time. Security for the games was also insured by having "spotters" surveil the area continuously.

The County Sheriff was present at the opening of the gambling establishment and was overheard informing Nesline and his associates that if he received any complaints concerning gambling, he was going to raid the establishment. Apparently, complaints were lodged, probably from the Feds, and three days after the new club's opening, it was raided by Maryland authorities. Subsequent to the raid, the St. Mary's County Sheriff and Maryland State Police arrested Joe Nesline and Charlie Tourine. Frank "Lefty" Rosenthal, Eugene "Jabba" Corsi, Duke Zeibert and other gamblers were also arrested. The actor George Raft was present at the club but only questioned, the others were released on bond. The raid in Maryland stemmed from an investigation initiated against Joe at the Amber Club in D.C. The case was later taken over by the Feds.

Joe again retained the powerful D.C. law firm of Edward Bennett Williams for his defense counsel. Attorneys Vincent Fuller and Barbra Babcock were assigned as his defense. While the case languished in the federal court system, Joe Nesline and his codefendants continued with various endeavors. Joe had many more irons in the fire in the States and across the seas. Joe would periodically return to the District to consult with his attorneys. In May of 1965, Joe, Charlie and others were indicted by a federal grand jury in D.C. for operating an illegal gambling operation at the Amber Club. Joe and Charlie were also indicted for transporting gambling equipment across state lines. George Raft and Duke Zeibert were not charged but were called as grand jury witnesses. Only Joe Nesline and Charlie Tourine were eventually found guilty of violating Maryland gambling laws. They avoided any prison time and paid $9,500 in court fees and agreed to stay out of St. Mary's County. By July of 1967, all other charges were dismissed against Joe and Charlie. The jury was hopelessly deadlocked on the charges and the Judge dismissed the case. After the dismissal, Joe threw a victory party at Duke Zeibert's restaurant.

16

"Legal Eagles"

The Lawyers

Over the years Joe Nesline's chosen profession required the retainment of legal services, beginning with Charlie Ford and his "Fifth Street" lawyers and later with Edward Bennett Williams of the high-profile Washington, D.C. law firm of Williams & Connelly. Edward Williams also defended high profile mobsters and Mob associates like Chicago Outfit hitman Felix "Milwaukee Phill" Alderisio and Teamster Boss James Riddle "Jimmy" Hoffa. Williams had controlling interests in the Baltimore Orioles baseball team and the Washington Redskins football team. One of Joe Nesline's associate lawyers with the Williams & Connolly Law Firm was Vincent Fuller. In 1957, Fuller won an acquittal for Jimmy Hoffa on charges of bribery and obstruction of justice. Later he went on to represent President Ronald Reagan's assailant John Hinkley.

After the Amber Club trial, Joe's co-counsel with Vincent Fuller was Barbara Babcock who began a social relationship with Nesline. Later on, Ms. Babcock became Assistant Attorney General and head of the Civil Rights Division of the U.S. Justice Department during the Carter Administration. In February 1978, an article appeared in the Chicago Tribune describing the social relationship between Barbara Babcock and top Washington Mob boss Joe Nesline. Based on the report, Ms. Babcock stated she would give up her long-time relationship with Joe.

During the time the Amber Club case was pending in D.C. federal court, Charlie Tourine also retained Barbara Babcock to defend his son Chuckie Delmonico who had been charged with bank robbery in Evansville, Indiana. Charlie "The Blade" remarked to his lawyer "Chuckie don't have the guts to rob a bank." Ms. Babcock successfully defended Chuckie. He was misidentified as the perpetrator of the crime and was actually innocent of the charge. Chuckie had spontaneously changed his name from Tourine to Delmonico one night when police officers threw him against an alley wall and demanded his identification. Looking up, his eyes lit upon the glowing neon of Delmonico's, the famous steakhouse he had been headed to in lower Manhattan. Chuckie Delmonico himself was eventually prosecuted for other crimes, and died in the federal penitentiary in Atlanta while serving a long sentence.

After her stint as Assistant Attorney General at the U.S. Justice Department, Barbara Babcock would go on to be the director of the District of Columbia Public Defender Service and the first female law professor at Stanford University. In 2016, she released an autobiographical book titled "Fish Raincoats: A Woman Lawyer's Life." In a segment of her book Barbara Babcock writes about her personal and legal relationship with Joe Nesline and other infamous characters. The legal trailblazer Barbara Allen Babcock died in 2020 at her Stanford, Connecticut home.

17

"Politics and Parties"

Partying with JFK and the Rat Pack

Frank Sinatra escorting Jacqueline Kennedy

at the D.C. National Guard Armory

January 19, 1961, at a gala the night before

John F. Kennedy's Inauguration

(photo Associated Press)

During the 1960 presidential campaign John F. Kennedy leveraged his family's connections with the overworld and underworld into a successful run to the White House. Frank Sinatra served as Kennedy's conduit into all these spheres of influence for support. The Rat Pack played a pivotal role in JFK's razor thin margin

86

of victory. Sinatra barnstormed the country stumping for Kennedy and helping him raise money. The JFK campaign used Sinatra's "High Hopes" song as its theme music. The night before the 35th President-Elect was sworn in on January 20, 1961, Sinatra hosted a star-studded celebration for JFK at the D.C. Armory. Featured performers at the celebration were Jimmy Durante, Nat King Cole and other celebrities. Sinatra escorted Jacqueline Kennedy to her box at the gala.

President Kennedy celebrated his victory by carousing the night away with Sinatra's Rat Pack and other celebrities as well as mobsters from New York and Chicago. In the in-between times of law enforcement's raids on Nesline's operations, one of the parties in honor of JFK's inauguration was held at Joe's Spartan American Club. Sinatra and George Raft were at the opening of Joe Nesline's new establishment, the Amber Club. According to a February 1961 FBI report, while at the Amber Club, Sinatra and George Raft lost heavily at the craps table. Raft was heard saying he had never seen a larger craps game outside of Las Vegas or Reno. FBI Director J. Edgar Hoover presented surveillance photos to JFK's brother Robert Kennedy of Sinatra's and Raft's carousing with Joe Nesline and other Mob figures. This eventually led to President Kennedy's disassociation with Frank Sinatra. However, JFK and Bobby Kennedy were still attending events together with Sinatra and Peter Lawford. They all attended a benefit dinner for Los Angeles' Cedars-Sinai Hospital in July of 1961.

An alternate version as to why Sinatra fell out of favor with the Kennedys was revealed under oath by former Washington D.C. Metropolitan Police Inspector

Joseph W. "Joe" Shimon who, it appears had friends in low places. He maintained close connections with the CIA, FBI as well as Chicago Mob boss Sam Giancana and Johnny Roselli. According to Shimon, Hoover had gone to Bobby Kennedy with some of the latest audio from Giancana's bugged telephones. Hoover played the selected tape and they listened to Giancana and Sinatra in private conversation. Giancana demanded Sinatra use his influence with the Kennedys to get him relief from the government. Sinatra told Giancana he was working on it. Sinatra was having an affair with the president's sister, Patricia Kennedy Lawford, the wife of actor and "Rat Pack" member Peter Lawford, to get her to use her influence on the brothers. From then on Sinatra was out. The Attorney General Robert Kennedy would go on to plan an aggressive prosecution of the Mob in federal court. That aggressive stance against the Mob ended with the assassination of JFK. Not until the enactment of the RICO statute in the 1970s, would the Feds pick up where Bobby left off.

18

"Hoodlum Sea"

Expansion into Cuba

Fulgencio Batista, Thelma Lansky, Meyer Lansky

Havana, Cuba 1946

(photo First published in Cuba 1947)

Meyer Lansky, Charles "Lucky" Luciano, and Santo Trafficante had always recognized Cuba as the ideal location for an offshore base of operations. Lansky was the first to establish a relationship with Batista. In Cuba, Fulgencio Batista y Zaldívar was the Mob's main man. A sergeant in the military, Batista took over control of Cuba in a coup in 1933 and reigned for ten years. In 1933, Lansky' first business deal with Batista was over molasses in order to make rum for the Mob's newly legalized distilleries. The dictator resigned from office in 1943 and lived the high life as Lansky's Florida neighbor. Batista returned to power in Cuba in

1952 until 1960. In 1952, Batista appointed Lansky as Cuba's director of gambling reform. Lansky cleaned up the island's bad reputation for rigged casino gambling. This would lead to an expansion in the gaming and entertainment industry in Cuba unlike anything seen before.

It all started with the casinos, which were mostly located inside the best hotels in town. Lansky's Hotel Nacional and Hotel Riviera had the swankiest casinos. Designed by internationally renowned architect Igor Boris Polevitzky, the casino floor was oval, with luxurious wall-to-wall carpeting, gold leaf walls and custom-designed gold and crystal chandeliers. In the center of the casinos were the gaming tables with roulette, craps, blackjack and baccarat, with rows of slot machines lining the walls. The bars were located off the casino floor and were the hotel's venues for live entertainment. All the hotels had a nightclub that became the center of a fabulous entertainment scene, with hot Latin jazz orchestras, showgirls with elaborate floor shows, and many top entertainers from the United States. These casinos generated a huge cash-flow for the Mob.

Outside these official worlds of casino gambling and live entertainment was a lively underworld of bordellos, sex shows, private high-stakes card games, and access to narcotics. This put the Mob in a position to use their political and underworld connections to make Cuba one of their narcotics smuggling points where the drugs could be stored before they continued on to Canada and the United States via Montreal and Florida.

Between the 1929 Atlantic City Mob Conference and the 1957 Apalachin Mafia Summit, there was the Havana Conference of 1946, an historic meeting of Mob leaders in Cuba. The conference was held during the week of December 22, 1946, to discuss important Mob policies and business interests. The Conference was attended by delegations representing Mafia families and Jewish Syndicate members throughout the United States. The Havana Conference was considered the most important Mob summit since the Atlantic City Conference. The Cuban summit was held at Hotel Nacional which was owned by Meyer Lansky and his silent partner, Cuban president Fulgencio Batista. It was around the time of these Syndicate meetings that Lansky allegedly made the famous comment that the American Mafia was "bigger than United States Steel," at one time the world's largest corporation. The quote was also used by the fictional Hyman Roth in the film "The Godfather II." Lansky was the inspiration for the Roth character portrayed by Lee Strassberg.

Meyer Lansky organized the 1946 Mob summit in Havana on orders from Lucky Luciano, who was exiled from the United States to Italy. Luciano then received a sealed envelope which contained three words, "December-Hotel Nacional." With an Italian passport issued in his real name, Salvatore Lucania, he was able to visit the Western Hemisphere and meet with criminal associates from the U.S. In October, Luciano traveled from Italy to Venezuela, Mexico and finally Cuba. Meyer Lansky greeted his old friend on his arrival. To welcome Luciano to Cuba and acknowledge his continued authority within the Mob, all the conference invitees brought Luciano cash envelopes. These "Christmas Tributes" totaled more than $200,000, the equivalent of $3 million today. The official cover story for the Havana Conference was that the mobsters were attending a gala party with Frank Sinatra as the entertainment. Sinatra flew to Havana with Al Capone's cousins, the Fischetti brothers.

The most pressing items on the conference agenda were the leadership and authority within the New York Mafia, the Mob-controlled Havana casino interests, the narcotics operations, and the West Coast operations of Benjamin "Bugsy" Siegel, especially the new Flamingo Hotel and casino in Las Vegas. Suspected of skimming from the Flamingo building project, and with millions of dollars in overruns, Siegel was eventually gunned down in his Beverly Hills home in June 1947, by hitman Frankie Carbo.

19

"Exiled"

"Lucky Luciano"

Salvatore Lucania

Charles "Lucky" Luciano

(photo American Mafia History)

Salvatore Lucania was born in Sicily in 1897, but the future brains of the New York mafia took the name Charles Luciano after his parents disowned him for dealing heroin. By the 1930s he was known as "Lucky" Luciano. One theory for his moniker was his remarkable luck in surviving a savage beating. Luciano's face was a bloody mess, his eyes so swollen he could barely see out of them, his neck and throat slashed. Luciano had been "taken for a ride," in quintessential Mob parlance, beaten and left for dead in a wooded field in Staten Island, New York. As a result of the attack, he had a deep scar on one side of his face and a permanently drooping eyelid. The real reason for Luciano's nickname came from his childhood friendships with Yiddish speaking kids calling Salvatore Lucania "Lukie" which eventually became "Lucky".

April 1931 ended 14 months of bloody conflict on the streets of New York between a younger Americanized generation of Italian gangsters and the older "Unione Siciliana," (the Sicilian Mafia). The conflict was known as the Castellammarese War, named after a Mafia stronghold town in Sicily. When hostilities ended, Luciano emerged as the Boss of what would eventually be the Genovese Crime Family. In that same year an ambitious 28-year-old Thomas E. Dewey was appointed as Chief Assistant United States Attorney for New York. At the time, Jewish gangsters outnumbered the Italian Mafia. After a series of successful prosecutions of Jewish gangsters including Dutch Shultz, Dewey set his sights on Luciano. Ironically, unknown to Dewey, Luciano probably saved the prosecutor's life. After Dewey shut down Dutch's operations, Dutch swore to put a hit on Dewey. Luciano intervened, considering the hit a bad idea and bad for business. He believed the heat would be too much. Luciano instead called for a hit on Dutch, and, in 1935 Dutch was gunned down in the toilet of a New Jersey Chop House. In 1936, Luciano was convicted by Dewey for operating a prostitution racket and was sentenced to 30 to 50 years.

A path towards an early release for "Lucky" Luciano began at 2:30 pm on February 9th 1942 when a fire broke out on the ship the USS Lafayette docked at the end of West 48th Street on Pier 88 in New York Harbor. Despite the efforts of the largest gathering of emergency services on American soil at the time, a mighty asset in America's war effort was lost.

"On the Water Front:"

During World War II New York City ports were a major marshalling point for outbound convoys of war goods. In February 1942, the Allied war effort was struck a $5 million blow when a suspicious inferno devoured the French-built super-liner Normandie while it was being retrofitted for military use. Seized from the Nazi collaborating Vichy French and renamed the USS Lafayette, the militarized liner was fast and capable of carrying 10,000 troops and munitions. The Navy suspected Nazi foul play, but the official Navy report as to the cause of the inferno was sparks from a welder's torch igniting greasy rags. The loss of the vessel highlighted a weakness in America's strongest port. If enemy agents could paralyze this lifeline, it could mean a catastrophic defeat for American forces.

At the outset of the war, Mussolini's Italy was allied with Germany. Of particular concern to Naval Intelligence officers was the fact that large numbers of the work force in the New York ports were of Italian ancestry. This included the fishing fleet, the wholesale and retail fish markets, the teamsters and the longshoremen. There was great concern that some of these workers could be Axis sympathizers who might engage in sabotage or provide intelligence on ship movements to the enemy. Within the first five months of 1942, torpedoes from Nazi submarines sent more than 100 ships to the bottom. Many of those vessels were sunk just 60 miles off the coast of Long Island, New York. Naval Intelligence feared that American fishing vessels were assisting these marauding Nazi U-boats. The Navy suspected these fishermen were either ex-rumrunners or Axis sympathizers on the waterfront. It became necessary to use every possible means necessary to prevent sabotage.

The American Mafia maintained an utter dominance of the docks. Union officials and people in illegal operations along the waterfront had more influence on the docks than the shipping officials themselves. Only the Mob had the power to hunt down the guilty party. The Navy wanted the Mob's help, but were wary of enlisting the aid of such a criminal organization.

After weeks of intensive research, the Intelligence officers discovered that the Mafia represented the most antifascist organization in the world. Under Benito Mussolini's savage purges, Sicilian Mafiosi were bombed, machine-gunned, arrested and tortured in droves. Many of the original members of the American Mafia had fled their homeland because of the attacks. The vast majority of the Italian immigrants were from the poorer rural south of the Italian peninsula and Sicily. For those new immigrants to the new world, an Italian national identity was lower down the totem pole of their psyche. By 1942, Italy as one sovereign nation was barely 80 years old. The unification of the various federations of the Italian peninsula only worsened the condition of the population of the rural South with most taxes and resources going to benefit the industrial North. Two million Southern Italian immigrants arrived in New York between 1900 and 1914. Many of the uneducated new arrivals were not fluent in the Italian language, they mainly spoke their regional dialects and identified themselves as Sicilian or Neapolitan, Abruzzo or Calabrian.

"PROJECT UNDERWOLD:"

One of the most unusual episodes of the war remained a secret until 1977. Author Rodney Campbell, while organizing New York Governor Thomas E. Dewey's archives uncovered the classified 1954 Herlands investigative report. The 101-page report summarized over 3,000 pages of testimony that detailed the Navy's involvement in "Project Underworld." The project was led by U.S. Navy Commander Charles Haffendon operating out of the former Times Square Astor Hotel. The Commander assembled a dedicated team of agents with diverse skills, many of them Italian-Americans who were versed in the Italian dialects spoken by the underworld. It was, in essence, another "Italian Squad." All members of the unit were U.S. Naval reservists. The unit was headed by Lieutenant Anthony "Tony" Marsloe, a lawyer who was raised by an Italian family and was fluent in Italian, French and Spanish and had worked for Special Prosecutor Thomas Dewey in his crusade against organized crime. Other members of the unit were Lieutenant Joseph Titolo, a former bootlegger now in charge of breaking and entering operations, Lieutenant Paul Alfieri, a safecracker and Lieutenant James "Jim" Murray a former police officer, who had learned the Italian language from his Italian mother.

With input from these officers, Haffendon called on New York District Attorney Frank Hogan to seek permission to contact some of the Mob figures who were key players in the waterfront unions and enlist their support in securing the ports of New York and New Jersey. To guarantee cooperation on the waterfront they needed to be told to cooperate by the "Big Boss" Lucky Luciano, who was incarcerated and would not be eligible for parole until 1956. Meyer Lansky made the original approach to seek Luciano's cooperation. Unlike the Mafia, the Navy never questioned Lansky's patriotism. Luciano agreed, despite the fact that he was repeatedly told that he would receive no favorable treatment in return for his cooperation. Project Underworld was an immediate success; troublemakers were removed, and the word was put out to report anything suspicious and to cooperate fully with the Navy and with the war effort. If there were any problems, Luciano was to be notified, and he would ensure the problems stopped. There never were any problems, there was no sabotage, no work stoppages, no slow-downs and the ports remained secure for the entire duration of the war. The U.S. Navy would also use Luciano's assistance in gaining allies in Sicily in advance of the planned invasion of Italy.

"OPERATION HUSKY"

In May 1943, the Commander of Naval Forces Northwest African Waters, wrote to the Director of Naval Intelligence requesting Italian/Sicilian speaking officers be assigned to his staff to help him plan the upcoming invasion of Sicily. In response to the request, a team of volunteers headed by Lieutenant Anthony Marsloe responded. Naval Intelligence had been collecting information on Sicily for some time and with Lucky Luciano and the Mob's influence, they were able to obtain points of contact on the island. Hundreds of Sicilians were interviewed and the information was collated and plotted on a large map. Armed with this information the team immediately set sail for the Mediterranean to join the US Naval Forces. When the Sicily invasion kicked-off, Marsloe's team landed with the first wave and immediately went inland to contact sympathetic natives who might be able to provide critical intelligence. With the assistance of Sicilian Mafia contacts, they were able to obtain maps of minefields, schematics of German defensive positions and codebooks.

The team also participated in the Salerno and Anzio invasions. In Rome they rescued an Italian Admiral who had helped the Allies. In Florence they located Mussolini's personal archives at a secret villa on Lake Garda. The team members all received Legions of Merit for their heroic work. Several received Bronze Stars and medals awarded by the Italian underground. Their exploits would not have been possible without the contacts provided them by the New York City Mob and the local Mafia in Sicily.

In May 1945, after the surrender of Germany, "Lucky" Luciano's lawyer, drew up a petition to then New York Governor Thomas E. Dewey, requesting executive clemency for his client based on the premise that he already served ten years of his 30-to-50-year sentence and he had helped the Navy and the nation in their fight against the Axis. In January 1946, acting on the advice of the Executive Clemency Board of the New York State Department of Corrections, Governor Dewey granted a special commutation of Luciano's sentence and Luciano was immediately deported to Italy.

Files on "Project Underworld" and "Operation Husky" in Washington D.C. and the New York Naval District were ordered destroyed. From that point on, the official position of the Navy was "we have no record of any such cooperation." This remained the Navy's position throughout the remainder of the 1940s and into the 1970s.

The December 7, 1998 issue of Time magazine, "Builders & Titans," listed Charles "Lucky" Luciano in the top 100 most influential business geniuses of the century. A reporter once asked Luciano if he would do it all again. "I'd do it legal," Lucky replied. "I learned too late that you need just as good a brain to make a crooked million as an honest million. These days you apply for a license to steal from the public. If I had my time again, I'd make sure I got that license first."

20

"The Mob's Money-Man"

Meyer Lansky

Maier Suchowljansky

Meyer Lansky

(photo Mob Museum)

In 2012, the FBI released nearly 3,000 pages of files on Mob bosses. One file in particular concerned Meyer Lansky and his relationship with Joe Nesline. During his post-Cuba years, Lansky was involved with running Mob money through his Miami Beach motel, The Singapore. The cash from casinos and gambling junkets from Europe and the Caribbean went to Swiss banks and into Mob fronts in the United States and ensured that everyone got their fair share. Lansky wanted Nesline to take over this job upon his death. Lansky had other close associates, but they were used more as bagmen. Nesline was a more trusted associate in terms of being introduced to and working with Lansky's Mob connections that facilitated the filtering of illegal gambling money into the United States economy.

Meyer Lansky, along with "Lucky" Luciano, were the most important figures in the development of organized crime in 20th century America. Lansky immigrated with his family from Imperial Russia in 1911. Lansky's career began with the pre-Prohibition days of the New York City rackets. He later formed the violent bootlegging "Bug-Meyer Gang" with his friend "Bugsy" Siegel. In the 1930s, Lansky and his gang stepped outside their usual criminal activities to break up rallies held by the pro-Nazi German-American Bund. Lansky recalled a particular rally in the German-American neighborhood of upper Manhattan that he and his gang disrupted; "The stage was decorated with a swastika and a picture of Adolf Hitler. The speakers started ranting. There were only fifteen of us, but we went into action. We threw some of them out the windows. Most of the Nazis panicked and ran out. We chased them and beat them up. We wanted to show them that Jews would not always sit back and accept insults." Their gang later joined up with Charlie Luciano and went on to the development of Las Vegas and Havana as "open cities" for the Mob. Lansky also controlled casinos in the Bahamas and Europe. Reportedly, Lansky had a controlling interest in a Swiss-based bank through which he laundered the Mob's profits.

In the 1940s, Lansky began investing in Las Vegas casinos, and assigned his friend "Bugsy" Siegel to oversee construction of the Flamingo Hotel. "Bugsy" Seigel hired Del Webb, the owner of a construction company, as the general contractor for the Flamingo Hotel and Casino and also to make alterations in Bugsy's home in Nevada. When Del Webb realized that the home he was renovating belonged to the notorious killer he grew nervous. When he saw the panicked look on the face Del Webb Bugsy told him: "Del, don't worry, we only kill each other." Ironically for Seigel that was a true and prophetic statement. The project's cost overruns ballooned and some of Lansky's fellow Mob investors were unhappy. Some believed that Siegel, who also tightly controlled income from the Los Angeles "telephone race wire" providing sports results to bookie parlors and casinos, was stealing from their investment. In 1947, "Bugsy" Seigel was gunned down while inside the Beverly Hills home of his girlfriend, Virginia Hill. Lansky was a power as a Jewish member of the Syndicate, but he had no veto power over the decision of the Italian led Commission. Lansky and his associates immediately took over the Flamingo upon Siegel's death, and the property generated income for Lansky and others for decades.

Delbert Eugene "Del" Webb was an American real-estate developer, and a co-owner of the New York Yankees baseball club. He is known for founding and developing the retirement community of Sun City, Arizona and for many works of his firm, the Del E. Webb Construction Company. During World War II, "Del" received many military contracts, including the construction of the Poston War Relocation Center near Parker, Arizona, which interned over 17,000 Japanese Americans.

Lansky's gambling operations ran into a multimillion-dollar disaster with the Cuban Revolution of 1959. Rebel leader Fidel Castro nationalized all of Lansky's casino interests on the island. Lansky also suffered from crackdowns on illegal gambling in the United States, including casinos in Florida. Despite his efforts to conceal income, in 1970 Lansky was indicted on federal tax evasion charges. He and his family fled to Israel under the Jewish nation's "right of return," but that right did not extend to criminals and he was asked to leave. Lansky returned to the United States and was arrested in the Miami International Airport. Lansky was ultimately acquitted of all charges.

Later in his life, Lansky started keeping diaries. He wrote in one of the spiral-bound accountant's notebooks a fascinating and provocative glimpse of the moral musings of a mobster on America's double standards of right and wrong. In his diaries, Lansky blasted Establishment-types who got rich through legalized gambling as "swindlers" and "hypocrites." The gangster angrily complained that while he and other men who created the gambling industry in America were branded as criminals, leaders of the "Establishment" who made millions running legalized gambling operations were praised as successful businessmen. When the condemnation of gambling by respectable society and the government ended, Lansky wrote; "Only when the Hiltons, the Loews, the Sheratons, the Rockefellers entered the gambling fraternity and many more from 'Who is Who.' When the Establishment doesn't earn the profits in gambling, they say it is run by gangsters, it is immoral." His bitterness leaping off the page. "All this takes on a different twist when it's operated by the big corporations. We speak of gambling as though it is a commodity one time, and a sin another time. I agree that gambling isn't the most moral habit when you become addicted to it," Lansky concluded, "for that matter what is good when you abuse it"? But Lansky said that as long as people want to gamble, someone will provide gambling opportunities. The only question is who that someone will be.

"They weren't really criminals. Who did they kill?
Seriously, look back and see who did they kill?
They didn't kill an innocent person on the street,
they didn't rob, they didn't loot.
They helped build this country."
Quote from Sandra Lansky, Meyer Lansky's daughter

21

"From Hell's Kitchen to Hollywood"

George Raft

George Raft

(photo Hollywood's Golden Age)

By 1957, the Mob had turned Havana, Cuba into the hottest entertainment scene on the planet. It was a place where movie stars and gangsters merged. It was therefore logical that the Mob needed someone who embodied all those traditions. That person was George Raft, a tough guy who could walk the walk. In November of 1957, George Raft was hired as the public face of the Trafficante owned Hotel Capri casino and nightclub in Havana. With Raft presiding at the Casino de Capri, the biggest stars of the day flooded into Havana. The Island had arrived as the place to be.

George Raft (Ranft) was born around 1900, and grew up in a poor German immigrant family in Hell's Kitchen, at the time one of the roughest, meanest areas of New York City. In his youth, he showed a great interest and aptitude for dancing. He left home while still a young teenager, and by 1920 he had been an electrician, a professional boxer racking up 9 wins 2 losses and 2 draws and a minor league baseball player. But what he excelled at was dancing, and that, combined with his dark good looks and sharp dressing, made him a local favorite at such spots as "Texas" Guinan's the El Fey Club. While working the New York City nightclubs as a "Taxi Dancer," he befriended future silent film idol Rudolph Valentino who was working at the same venues. Raft even toured Europe with his dancing and helped popularize the tango in Paris, Vienna, Rome and London.

During prohibition he found work as a Broadway actor and dancer, while at the same time running booze for Owney "The Killer" Madden's "Gopher Gang." During this time his circle of friends included stars like Mae West, the writer Damon Runyon and gangsters Arnold Rothstein, Bugsy Siegel and Charlie "Lucky" Luciano. George Raft had a fierce sense of loyalty to the people he grew up with and worked with and he never apologized for his associations with them.

In 1928, Raft went to Hollywood to try his luck in the movies. Raft was urged to go to Hollywood by Speakeasy empresario and entertainer Mary Louise Cecilia "Texas" Guinan. His intimate knowledge of the gangster life eventually served him well on the silver screen. After the death of the silent era movie idol Rudolph Valentino, Hollywood producers approached Raft to take over Valentino's "Latin

Lover" movie roles. He turned down the offer, he thought it would be disrespectful to Valentino's memory and to his fans. His first big role was the coin-tossing henchman "Guino Rinaldo" in the 1932 movie "Scarface." His career was marked by numerous tough-guy roles, often as a gangster or a convict. During the 1940s, his acting roles became more sympathetic and heroic. During World War II, George Raft returned to England and performed for the British and American soldiers in London. He was very popular with the troops.

The believability with which he played these tough-guy roles, together with his lifelong associations with real-life gangsters, added to persistent rumors that he was also a gangster. This slightly shady reputation may have helped his popularity early on, but it made him somewhat undesirable to movie executives later in his career. After his movie career ended, his status as an international celebrity continued to benefit him in Havana and later in London.

Raft's mob connections once saved fellow gangster-film legend James Cagney's life. In his autobiography "*Cagney on Cagney*," the actor claimed his life was threatened by the Mob while he was president of the Screen Actors Guild and was trying to diminish organized crime's influence on the unions. Raft intervened with his gangster associates on Cagney's behalf, and was able to have the hit called off. It's said that Raft also did the same for Gary Cooper after the Western star's romantic dalliances earned him a spot on a mobster's hit list. Raft's fame magnified his influence, making him an idol of many of the era's actual gangsters. But for his part, Raft did what he could to distance himself from the Mob in the public eye, insisting that his gangland pals were merely acquaintances. Raft managed to dodge a life of crime while helping to establish the gangster film as a Hollywood mainstay that endures to this day.

By the 1950s, George Raft's movie career was dwindling. In 1955 Raft's old friends offered him a chance to buy a 2% share in the Flamingo Hotel in Las Vegas for $65,000 if he acted as entertainment director. Raft agreed, but was rejected for a gaming license because of "too many associations with underworld figures." He appealed, arguing he knew many gangsters, "but I never did business with any of them" and managed to get the decision overturned. In December 1955. He went to work at the hotel negotiating their show business deals.

In 1958 Raft was offered the same deal by Santo Trafficante Jr. to come to Cuba to work as a greeter at his and Meyer Lansky's Capri Casino in Havana. This ended when Fidel Castro took over the country and stamped out the casinos. The revolution started out as a kind of a combination celebration and riot all rolled into one. In the early morning of January 1, 1959 huge mobs of people started to flow through the streets of Havana making music and cheering revolutionary slogans. One of the first things they did was target the casinos. They went into a number of the hotels and trashed the casinos and dragged the gambling equipment out into the streets and set them on fire. In some casinos, the revolutionaries even herded pigs into the casinos to do what pigs do.

This was a clear example of the degree to which the casinos, the gambling and the whole presence of the Mob in Havana had become a source of resentment that eventually boiled over on the morning of January 1, 1959. George Raft was at the Capri Casino in Havana greeting people as usual the night the revolutionaries arrived. The crowd and the revolutionary guard stormed in to trash the casino, but Raft was determined to save the place. A woman who was leading the crowd halted the attack when she saw him and in English, she yelled "It's George Raft, the movie star!" He negotiated with them, arranged food for them and got them to leave without damaging the casino.

The revolution scene was depicted in the 1961 BioPic, "The George Raft Story." Ray Danton portrays the eponymous main character and the film co-starred Jayne Mansfield. George Raft parodied his gangster reputation in Billy Wilder's 1959 movie "Some Like It Hot," starring Tony Curtis, Jack Lemon and Marilyn Monroe. Raft also appeared in a prison scene Alka-Seltzer TV commercial along with tough-guy character actors Mike Mazurki and Robert Strauss. The one-minute spot that aired in the 1960s was rated one of the greatest TV Ads of all time.

"I've never been locked up, I've never taken a drink,
I've never hurt anybody, and I gave all my money away."
"So how come I got this bum reputation?"
George Raft

22

"Pirates of the Caribbean"

The Bahamas

In 1960, after the loss of Cuba as an income stream for the Mob, "Lucky" Luciano and Meyer Lansky started making plans to expand their operations further into the Caribbean. However, Luciano died of a heart attack in January 1962, at the Naples International Airport in Italy and Lansky had to continue on with the expansion plans without his childhood friend. Starting in 1962, Lansky set up a series of meetings held at the Mob associated Fontainebleau Hotel in Miami Beach, Florida. The purpose of the meetings was to discuss the plans for expanding gambling into the Bahamas and beyond. Among the attendees at these meetings were Joe Nesline, Charlie Tourine, Dino Cellini, Michael "Trigger Mike" Coppola and two North American expatriate Bahamian business developers, Wallace Groves and Louis Chesler. Also in attendance were long time Lansky gambling associates Charles Brudner, Max Courtney and Frank Ritter.

Following its opening in 1954, "Trigger Mike" Coppola made Miami's Fontainebleau Hotel his operating base, just as Frank Costello in New York used the Waldorf Astoria as a Mob headquarters. Coppola went by the name of Michael Kaplan to confuse any law enforcement investigators as he operated from a luxurious cabana, one of 250 that sat alongside the hotel's 6500 square foot pool. The Mob associated Fontainebleau Hotel was where the Mob and the CIA met to plan the assassination of Fidel Castro.

The Mob and their partners on the Bahamian Islands eventually discovered more riches than Christopher Columbus ever dreamed of. It was Columbus that named the island archipelago "Baja Mar" for the shallow waters surrounding the Islands. Author Ed Reid wrote in his 1970 book, "Bahamian Fragments, Bits and Pieces from the History of The Bahamas;" "Columbus didn't know it, but he did find a pot of gold at the end of the rainbow when he steered his little ships into the heart of what has become one of the greatest crime syndicate enterprises since Al Capone left Brooklyn and discovered Chicago. Capone had no connection with Columbus, of course, but their descendants share one thing in common: a place at the trough of gold where pigs and paladins are born, weaned and grow to maturity—the West Indies. Laved on the north by the Atlantic Ocean and on the south by the warm waters of the Caribbean Sea, this ancient haunt of pirates is the new playground of the Mob."

Soon after Fidel Castro's "26th of July Movement" drove out the Mob's hold on Havana, Cuba, the Mob soon regrouped and went to some of the smaller islands in the Caribbean. Meyer Lansky became the Mob's point man for the move. Lansky set up the plan to turn The Bahamas into the Mob's new tropical paradise away from the Feds, and soon found willing partners to achieve this dream in the community of Freeport on the Grand Bahama Island of The Bahamas.

23

"Boy Wonder of Wall Street"

Wallace Groves

Wallace Groves

(photo Bahamas News Archives)

Meyer Lansky picked the Grand Bahama Island as the site for a new plush casino resort. He used front-men, starting with Virginia born, Wallace Groves, "Boy Wonder of Wall Street," as the first ex-pat partner to get the ball rolling. During the 1930s Wallace Groves had become a very successful financier in New York City with eventual ties to the Mafia. He served time in prison in 1941 after a stock swindle conviction. He moved to The Bahamas in 1955 and made an agreement with the Bahamian government to develop land and create jobs on the Grand Bahama Island. This Island was the ugliest and least promising of all the habitable islands in the Bahamas. Groves opened a lumber and sawmill business which almost deforested the Island. In the process he managed to acquire half the property on the island and converted it into the community of "Freeport."

Within the community of Freeport, Wallace Groves built big, garish hotels, with casinos that looked like Arabian harems, an old English pub with busty wenches, a shopping bazaar, girlie shows direct from Las Vegas, discothèques and a scuba club. Groves had a shipping tycoon associate, Daniel Keith Ludwig, who developed a port on Grand Bahama Island. Groves leased his hotels to Morris Lansburgh who had controlling interests in Hotels in Miami Beach. Lansburgh was also one of Meyer Lansky's front-men. By the early 1960s, Groves' businesses almost went bankrupt until a Canadian businessman, Lou Chesler, invested $12 million to set up the Grand Bahama Development Company (Devco) and gave Wallace Groves 50 per cent of Devco's stock.

Another businessman who tried to get rich in the Bahamas in 1959 was Huntington Hartford, one of the world's richest men, who inherited and ran A&P supermarkets. He bought the small Hog Island near Nassau and re-named it Paradise Island. He spent $30 million building luxury hotels there but soon discovered he could not make a profit without a casino. By the 1960s, Hartford gave up and sold Paradise Island to a paint company that would eventually become Resorts International Incorporated.

24

"Toronto Tycoon"

Louis A. Chesler

Louis A. Chesler

(photo Grand Bahama Museum)

Lansky's second ex-pat partner was Louis A. "Lou" Chesler, a Canadian businessman who was involved with the Mafia stretching back to at least 1942. Michael "Trigger Mike" Coppola was one of Chesler's Mob associates. Among Chesler's specialties was fencing stolen securities thru Switzerland and the Bahamas. In 1958 Meyer Lansky provided much of the investment capital for Chesler's Miami International Airport Hotel. Chesler and Lansky were involved in a number of Canadian mining deals and they also operated nightclubs in Miami Beach. Lou Chesler owned a Tampa, Florida based paint manufacturing business, the "Mary Carter Paint Company." With Wallace Groves providing the land and

Lou Chesler providing his Canadian connections and financing, the way was smoothed for Lansky's eventual construction of Hotels and Casinos in Freeport.

Lou Chesler's initial $12 million investment in The Bahamas came from his ownership of a small Canadian television production company called "Seven Arts." In 1967 Seven Arts bought Jack L. Warner's stock in Warner Brothers (WB) for $32 million. Seven Arts merged with WB and became Warner Bros–Seven Arts. After a series of deals which involved Frank Sinatra, the company would eventually become WarnerMedia, a multinational mass media and entertainment conglomerate. Chesler eventually purchased Paradise Island from supermarket magnate Huntington Hartford. It was about 2,000 feet off the shoreline from Nassau Island in the Bahamas. Resorts International Hotel/Casino was later built on Paradise Island.

Meyer Lansky and The Grand Bahama Development Company (Devco) spent the next three years negotiating the purchase of a large tract of land on the Grand Bahama Island and oversaw the construction of the Grand Lucayan Beach Hotel and Casino Corporation. Along with the Hotel/Casino, roads, sewers and stores for the city of Freeport were also built. In the early 1960s, construction began on the lavish, 250-room Lucayan Beach Hotel even before a Certificate of Exemption for gambling was granted, since gambling was illegal in the Bahamas. In 1963 Chesler received the certificate made out in the name of Bahamas Amusements, Ltd. The Mob was now back in business! The initial certificate stipulated that casino employees be citizens of the British Commonwealth and specifically excluded American personnel. Since Lou Chesler was a Canadian national, he carried none of the onus of the American gangster image. Lansky came up with the syndicate know-how of casino operations to attract, cater to, and extract the financial limits of the tourists. The Lucayan Beach Hotel/Casino opened for business before the end of 1963.

Casino Gambling became the most important tourist industry development in the Bahamas. When the Lucayan Hotel and Monte Carlo Casino opened, the plan was to operate gambling on the level of the ornate gambling palaces of Monaco. However, the initial opening was a big bust. The jet setters and high rollers failed to show, the Monte Carlo room remained empty. Chesler and Groves quickly learned what the casino operators of Las Vegas and Reno knew, a successful operation of larger casinos must make its profits off of the little people, simply because there are many more of them than the jet setters. Subsequently, plans changed and Meyer Lansky and his crew were brought in. The ban on American personnel in the Freeport casino was not enforced and was all but forgotten. Among the crew brought in to work the Monte Carlo room of the Lucayan Beach Hotel were some of the same attendees that were at Meyer Lansky's meeting at the Fontainebleau Hotel, Dino Cellini, Charles Brudner, Max Courtney, Frank Reiter, Charlie Tourine, and Joe Nesline.

By 1968, with the Lucayan Beach Hotel and Monte Carlo Casino a financial success, the company formerly known as "Mary Carter Paints" was renamed Resorts International and relocated to the Bahamas. By 1974, thanks to the

117

defeat of a referendum that would have restricted gambling in New Jersey, Resorts International started to become active in Atlantic City. After the company purchased an option on 55 acres of boardwalk, Resorts' stock soared as it became the casino front-runner in Atlantic City.

25

"The Front-Men"

Brud, Moishe, Red Reed

(photo The Digital Philatelist)

The Lucayan Beach Hotel/Monte Carlo Casino was managed by Lansky's longest established gambling technicians; Red Ritter was general manager, Dino Cellini was craps supervisor, Max Courtney was the credit manager, and Charlie Brudner was his assistant. Joe Nesline and Charlie Tourine handled the gambling junkets from the United States to the Bahamas.

Charles Brudner aka "Charlie Brud," Max Courtney, real name Morris (Moishe) Schmertzlerand and Frank Ritter aka Frank Reid / Reiter / Red Reed first made their marks as close associates of bootlegger Dutch Shultz. When Shultz was machine-gunned by his rivals, Courtney and Ritter decided to take up a less

119

violent occupation. In the 1950s they set up a lay-off bookmaking operation in Canada, to relieve the pressure of large bets made in Las Vegas, Chicago and New York. The Royal Canadian Mounted Police soon arrested the two bookies and they were expelled from Canada. Courtney and Ritter spent a number of years taking bets in various gaming centers in the United States. They became the heaviest sports bookmakers in the country, eventually becoming fugitives from American justice for income tax evasion.

Although officially banned from the Bahamas casinos, all three men were granted asylum "as residents" in the Bahamas despite their fugitive status. An agreement was made that over a ten-year period, the three men would receive $2.1 million for a credit-card file they brought to the island when gaming first began. Thousands of well-heeled American gamblers were listed on the cards. The decision for the payments was made by the president of the Bahamas Amusements, Ltd. It was a business decision so the casinos would continue to function smoothly and the operation would not be sabotaged. Courtney and Ritter eventually ended up as executives of the Monte Carlo Room at the Lucayan Hotel in Freeport.

The American mobsters Joe Nesline and Charlie Tourine handled the gambling junket flights from the U.S. to the Bahamas. Junkets were invented in Las Vegas in the 1950s. The junkets were set up to attract players to specific casinos to gain their loyalty and engage them in play. In return the player would receive incentives; free travel, the best hotel rooms, entertainment and fine dining for

120

committing to play at that casino during their stay. Different junkets had different requirements for the player to earn the benefits. Joe Nesline and his wife Josephine as well as Joe's courier Heidi Rikan and a gambling lay-off operator named Gil Beckley were frequent weekend guests at the Lucayan Beach Hotel and Monte Carlo Casino whenever they stayed at their vacation homes in Miami Beach, Florida. Charlie Tourine along with Joe Nesline eventually looked after Ritchie "The Boot" Boiardo's gambling interests in Antigua and Curacao.

The Feds in the U.S. kept its pressure and surveillance on the Mob in the Caribbean. They were convinced the Mob was getting a big cut of casino profits. They believed 30% of the profits was going to Meyer Lansky and also to Mafia Bosses Stephen Magaddino of Buffalo, Angelo Bruno of Philadelphia, Frank Costello of New York, Santo Trafficante Jr. of Tampa, and Joe Adonis who had been deported to Italy. Based on pressure from the Feds, Dino Cellini was eventually investigated by the Bahamian government and expelled in March 1964. In January 1967, Bruder, Courtney and Ritter were also going to be expelled, however, the new El Casino Hotel opened the same month and the three fugitives were allowed to stay for two weeks. They were to give a graduate course in running the new casino to their replacements. The new box-men, stickmen, and pit bosses at the El Casino were also Lansky associates from way back.

26

"Sadistic by Nature"

Michael Coppola

Michael "Trigger Mike" Coppola

(photo Gangster Inc.)

Without a doubt, the cruelest and most sadistic attendee at Meyer Lansky's 1962 meeting at the Fontainebleau Hotel in Miami was Michael "Trigger Mike" Coppola. Whenever photographed he always had a sneer on his face with a temperament to match. Despite the gunman's rise to power, Coppola's personal life would be a source of ongoing problems throughout his life. Just like "Machinegun" Jack McGurn, Benjamin "Bugsy" Seigel and George "Mad Dog" Harding, Coppola was eventually disowned by the Mob, but unlike McGurn, Seigel and Harding, he was allowed to live the rest of his life in exile.

Born at the turn of the 20th century, "Trigger Mike" was a New York City mobster who came up through the mafia ranks at its earliest inception. He started his criminal career working for Ciro Terranova, the half-brother of Giuseppe Morello, the first Mafia boss of a New York crime family. Coppola gained a reputation as a sadistic and violent gunman during Prohibition. From February, 1930 to April, 1931, a violent power struggle occurred in New York City between Mafiosi from Sicily and American Mobsters. The conflict became known as the "Castellammarese War." When the dust settled, control of the Morello Family eventually went to Charles "Lucky" Luciano. Coppola then became a high-ranking member of the Luciano Family, which ultimately became the Genovese Family.

In 1936 Luciano was convicted on prostitution charges and underboss Vito Genovese fled the country on a murder charge. Coppola was left in charge of Luciano's criminal operations until the 1950s. His most lucrative operation was the Harlem numbers racket, worth over $1,000,000 a year. Many notorious mobsters like Anthony "Fat Tony" Salerno worked for Coppola as "muscle" in the early stages of their mob careers.

A major part of Coppola's strength and power base rested on the support he and other mobsters received from the congressman for East Harlem, Vito Marcantonio. They helped get him the votes for re-election, and he made sure things worked smoothly in their favor. Marcantonio was fighting a primary in 1946, but his position was being jeopardized by the actions of a Republican party captain named John Scottoriggio who worked for Marcantonio's Republican opponent Frederick Van Pelt Bryan. It was believed Scottoriggio had in his possession a record of voter names he intended to contest the morning of the elections. Coppola and his group decided that it would be a good thing if Scottoriggio's intention was quashed. On the morning of election day as he left his apartment, four men beat Scottorigio so badly he died in the hospital six days later. The police arrested an ex-con for physically menacing three of the Republican Congressional District workers on Election Day. The ex-con asked to see District Attorney Frank Hogan, offering him information on the men who were behind the attack. Hogan's detectives picked up Harlem's most feared racket boss, "Trigger Mike" Coppola as a material witness. The police went after other suspects and over 800 witnesses would be interviewed in the Scottorigio murder case including Coppola's wife Doris Lehman. The case was eventually dropped when many potential witnesses started disappearing just after "Trigger Mike" was arrested. Suspiciously, Doris died in child birth while awaiting trial for perjury. After the death of Scottorigio, the New York City Police Department assigned uniformed police officers to fixed posts at all polling places in the city on election day.

In 1947, Coppola made one of many deals that helped make him a very rich man. He invested in the Manhattan Cigarette Company, a firm founded in 1936 by 'Doc' Stacher, a close aide of Meyer Lansky, and Mike Lascari, a relative of Luciano's. The business, originally called the Public Service Tobacco Company, was the largest cigarette-vending machine business on the East coast. Coppola bankrolled at least two of South Florida's bookmaking heavies, and Lansky's 1962 Fontainebleau attendees, Frank Ritter and Max Courtney. He also cemented relationships with Lansky's partners and meeting attendees, real-estate developers Louis Chesler and Wallace Groves. Through them, he linked into gambling ventures via the Grand Bahamas company called Mary Carter Paints which morphed into Resorts International in 1968.

In 1955, Coppola married a young widowed mother named Ann Drahmann. She was born Ann Augustine in Cincinnati, Ohio, of Italian descent. Their wedding reception was held at the Beverly Hills Club, outside the Mob controlled town of Newport, Kentucky. She had been married to Charley Drahmann who managed another Mob controlled Newport, Kentucky club, the "Lookout House" Casino. Charley was killed in a plane crash near Atlanta in 1952 while on Mob business. Coppola moved his new bride into his Miami Beach home. With a gourmet kitchen, a full-sized pool in the backyard, housekeeper, cook and gardener, it should have been a perfect life for Ann Coppola, but it soon all went downhill. For the next five years Ann would be subjected to domestic abuse and beatings. As the abuse went on, Coppola showered his wife with jewelry, furs and presents just to show off and prove to people what a big shot he was.

In 1960, Coppola was one of eleven men officially listed in the Nevada State "Black Book," barring his entry into Nevada casinos. That same year, Ann Drahmann-Coppola filed for divorce, supposedly due to Coppola supplying drugs to her teenage daughter from her first marriage, and later agreed to testify against

Coppola in an income tax investigation. Trigger Mike's lifestyle was supported on a declared annual income of $15,000. Coppola ordered several gunmen to kidnap and assault his wife. Even though she was severely beaten and found on an isolated beach, Ann continued cooperating with the investigation. In April 1961, Coppola was indicted on four counts of income tax evasion. Coppola pleaded guilty and was fined $40,000 and sentenced to four years in prison.

After Coppola's imprisonment, Ann fled to Europe with $250,000 (over $2 million today) of the crime family's money. While staying in Rome, Italy, she sent a letter to the Internal Revenue Service, with certain portions addressed to then U.S. Attorney General Robert F. Kennedy, detailing the criminal activities of the Genovese Crime Family. The letter also alleged that she had proof that Mike Coppola had murdered his first wife. That proof was never revealed. Ann's letter was also addressed to the incarcerated Coppola. In 1962, Ann Augustine Drahmann-Coppola committed suicide in her Rome hotel room by taking an overdose of sleeping pills. In 1968, author Hank Messick published a book "Syndicate Wife: The True Story of Ann Drahmann Coppola." Following his release from Atlanta Federal Prison in 1963, Coppola was unable to regain his previous power and lived in obscurity until his death three years later.

27

"Across the Pond"

Benny Huntman

Benjamin Huntman (left) with former

Heavyweight Champion Jack Dempsey

(photo courtesy of Roger Huntman, Benny's son

For the book"Mafialand; How the Mob Invaded Britain"

By Douglas thompson

In 1961, the United Kingdom passed the Betting and Gaming Act which provided a legal basis for off-course betting and casinos. Overnight, illegal bookmakers who were raided by police once a year became legitimate. The Act was poorly worded and allowed almost anyone to open a casino in England. Within six months hundreds of betting shops were established.

Among the other attendees of Meyer Lansky's 1962 series of meetings at the Fontainebleau Hotel, were Angelo Bruno, Boss of the Philadelphia Mob, the infamous Kray Twins of London, as well as business and gaming representatives from the Bahamas and the United Kingdom. The purpose of one of these meetings was to take advantage of the recently enacted Betting and Gaming Act in the UK. Meyer Lansky saw London as the springboard to Europe and onward to the Middle East and Africa. Point men had been in place since World War II, to open up London to American style gaming. Using aliases and passports created in an apartment in West London, Joe Nesline and his partners Dino Cellini and Charlie Tourine got busy setting up casino operations in Europe starting with London. To begin the Mob expansion into London casinos, Joe Nesline kept close contact with Benny Huntman, a Londoner who had long standing ties to America's "Original Gangsters."

Benny Huntman was a British born Jewish boxing promoter and a former professional boxer. In 1925, he was on the same bill with American world heavyweight boxing champion Jack Dempsey for charity exhibition fights in Brighton, England. Benny was fascinated with Dempsey and America. In 1926, during the Prohibition Era he arrived in New York City and got a job as a waiter in a "Speakeasy." After quickly dispatching a drunk and disorderly customer, Benny came to the attention of Frankie Carbo, who was a boxing promoter and a hired killer for the Mob. Through Carbo, Benny associated with the legendary gangsters of the time; Al Capone, "Lucky" Luciano, Meyer Lansky, "Bugsey Siegel, Jimmy "Blue Eyes" Alo and others. Carbo eventually eased Benny into the fight management game. Benny returned to England around 1930, and using his connections with American mobsters, started his career as a boxing promoter in London.

The discussion of plans for the expansion of gambling into Europe by American Organized Crime began in the 1950's between Frankie Carbo and Benny Huntman. With the collaboration of the London underworld the American Mafia took control of several prime locations in central London, including the Colony Sports Club. The management of the Colony Club was placed in the very capable hands of Dino Cellini and screen tough guy George Raft. Not long after, it became "George Raft's Colony Club." With London East End gangsters like Ronnie and Reggie Kray providing protection, The Colony Club was soon a big hit. The Kray twins were the subject of the 2015 BioPic crime thriller "Legend." English actor Tom Hardy portrayed the Kray Twins and Chaz Palminteri portrayed Philadelphia Mob Boss Angelo Bruno.

George Raft was very popular in England, he was fondly remembered from the war years when he entertained British troops. The veteran Hollywood star attracted glamour and cash when he arrived in the British capital. Every American film star, celebrity and sports figure who hit London came to dine and play at "George Raft's Colony Club. Officially listed as the casino director, Raft earned about $200 a week ($1,500 today) and a 5% stake in the club. He was provided with a swanky apartment and a maroon Rolls Royce with a chauffeur. Frank Sinatra made his mandatory appearance as well as many international film stars. The Colony Club became the "In Place" in London; the place to see and be seen. Frequent guests were Sophia Loren, Ursula Andress, Elizabeth Taylor and Richard Burton, Ari Onassis and Jackie Kennedy, Charlie Chaplin and other international celebrities. While filming in England, the entire cast of the war film "The Dirty Dozen," led by Telly Savalas, were regulars at the club. The sight of high rolling, oil-rich Arabs playing for high stakes was not uncommon. Even former Supreme Court Justice Earl Warren made his appearance.

The Colony Club Berkley Square – London
George Raft publicity photo
(photo Casino Chip and Token News)

For four years George Raft's Colony Club was the talk of the town until rival London gangsters, Governments on both sides of the "Pond," the Police and the

Press conspired to bring the Colony down and drive the Mob out of Britain. While returning to London from the States, both Dino Cellini and George Raft were declared undesirable aliens by Britain's Home Secretary and denied entry back into the United Kingdom.

Besides the numerous casinos in London that they were associated with, the Mob also had other European operations; The Grand Estoril Casino in Lisbon, Portugal, at the time the largest casino in Europe and The Hotel Lav Casino in Split, Yugoslavia (present day Croatia). In the 1970s Joe Nesline, Charlie Tourine along with his Steubenville partners Dino and Goffredo Cellini and the Lebanese/American Ayoub brothers Fred and Bobby ventured into casino operations in the Netherlands. With the financial backing from Jimmy "Blue Eyes" Alo of the Genovese family, they opened the Club Caballa Casino in Amsterdam. They had the Casa Rosso Club which was also the umbrella organization for European sex shops and brothels.

28

"The official verdict was suicide"

The Death of Freddie Mills

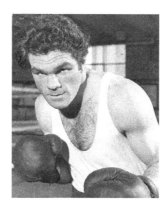

Frederick Percival Mills

Freddie Mills, 1948 World Light Heavyweight Champion

(photo London Daily Mail)

In 1965, the former British Light Heavyweight champion of the world, Freddie Mills was found dead in the back seat of his car, with a bullet through his eye. The official verdict was suicide.

Frederick Percival Mills born in 1919, was one of the first superstar sports personalities in Britain. Mills started boxing at the age of eleven. By seventeen Freddie was fighting in novice competitions and winning by knockout. At the outbreak of WWII Freddie Mills enlisted in the Royal Air Force in 1940 and also continued boxing professionally. His fights drew large crowds and his fighting spirit was a huge morale boost for the British forces. In 1942, he won the British and Empire light-heavyweight titles. His fights were featured on newsreels broadcast all over Britain. Mills gave the British public a hero to root for and he was a public face for the bravery of the boys on the front.

Benny Huntman had helped arrange Mills' 1948 title fight against Russian/American fighter Gus Lesnovich. After a brutal 15 round fight, Freddie Mills won the championship by decision. After sustaining so much punishment in the ring because of his boxing style, he retired in 1950. Still very popular to postwar Britain, Freddie tried his hand at show business. In 1957, Mills was in a British crime drama movie "Kill Me Tomorrow" with American film star, Pat O'Brien. Freddie next entered London's East End nightlife and went into the casino business.

On July 25, 1965, Mills was found dead in his car, parked in an alleyway behind his nightclub. A fairground rifle was found in the car with Mills, who had been shot through his right eye. He had told his staff that he was going for a nap in his car, something that he often did. His body was found by the doorman. An ambulance was not called until Freddie's wife arrived over an hour later. A week earlier Freddie had borrowed a .22 caliber rifle from a woman he knew who ran a shooting gallery. The rifle was not in working order when borrowed, it had apparently been repaired and was found in the car alongside him. The police were still not on the scene when ambulance personnel removed Freddie from his

133

car, disturbing the crime scene. Freddie's body was transported to the hospital where he was pronounced dead.

The investigation into his death initially assumed Freddie was murdered. However, the coroner's inquest determined that the angle of the bullet was consistent with a self-inflicted wound, and ruled the death a suicide. Family and friends did not accept the suicide verdict and in 1968, at the behest of Mills' wife, the case was reopened. There were some inconsistencies found regarding the death. Two shots had been fired in the car, one from a front seat which hit the nearside front door, and the one that had killed Mills while he was sitting in the back seat. Mills' body was found with his hands resting on his knees and the gun in a position out of Mills' reach. There were no fingerprints found on the rifle and the case was soon dropped. In 1970, the case was reopened again with inconclusive results.

In an August 2018, BBC (British Broadcasting Corporation) special, Roger Huntman, the son of Benny Huntman claims that his father masterminded the killing, in collusion with notorious American mobster Meyer Lansky. When Mills' nightclub began running up debts in 1965, he became desperate and attempted to blackmail Benny. Roger Huntman said "Freddie came to Benny's flat and said his nightspot was going "skint" (a British term for broke). He said "I need 2,500 pounds, Benny or I'm going under. I know who those guys are you're associating with. If you don't give me the money, I'm going to Fleet Street" (referring to the Royal Courts of Justice).

"Freddie tried to blackmail my father not thinking of the consequences." Benny Huntman was involved with Meyer Lansky who had a stake in the London casino business. Roger said he was instructed by his father to take a message to Mills, arranging a meeting to hand over the money on July 25th. In the early hours of July 26th, Roger said he was working in his father's casino. "At four in the morning, my father walked in with this old guy. I didn't think anything of it. It didn't cross my mind that anything could happen to Freddie. All of a sudden this massive guy, Italian American, he come over to my father and whispered in his ear, then he turned around and told the rest of the table, "Mills is dead. He's gone. He's finished. The old guy had a smirk on his face. Later I found out it was Meyer Lansky. Coincidence? I don't think so. He was there on the night Mills was shot."

Four months after the funeral of Frederick Percival Mills, Benny Huntman died of a heart attack.

29

"A Steubenville Phenom"

Dino Cellini

Dino Vincente Cellini

(photo Gaming Floor: Casino News and Operations Forum)

In 1987 Joe Nesline was interviewed by Frank Kuznik for Regardie Magazine concerning a 1967-68 Internal Revenue investigation for sports gambling and the Washington Redskins in which Joe Nesline was the target. Nesline told the D.C. reporter, "I think what little I know about gambling came from Dino. He was very good with figures. He could tell you what a cigarette smoked halfway down was worth. There is nobody I know who ever came close to Dino for being a gentleman and a nice man. He got a lot of bum raps." According to an FBI report, Dino Cellini was associated with Joseph F. "Joe" Nesline a Mafia boss who ran a sports betting operation in Washington, D.C.

Dino Vicente Cellini, born in 1914, was the son of Italian immigrants who grew up during the depression in the steel mill town of Steubenville, Ohio. A 1961 FBI file listed Benvenuto M. Cellini, father of Dino, Julia, Edward and Goffredo Cellini as residing at 8144 Eastern Avenue, N.W., Washington, D.C. Joe Nesline and Dino were friends for many years. In their younger days they both honed their gambling skills at Rex's Cigar Shop in Steubenville, Ohio and at Jimmy La Fontaine's Casino on the Maryland / DC border.

Before the Mob set up shop in Las Vegas after WWII, Steubenville was one of the Mob's largest hubs for games of chance, operating with little or no interference from local police or politicians. A regular system of gambling was run in the back rooms of clubs and restaurants. The Steubenville Cigar Shops were fronts for the Mob's rackets. Steel mill workers from Steubenville and Youngstown would frequent these shops after their shifts and blow their pay on craps and barboot, a Greek dice game, the games of choice at these places. The operators who ran the gambling halls would hire "mechanics," specialists in manipulating the dice. The mechanic would ward off undesirable customers, break winning streaks of lucky customers and hustle those with money to lose. Cellini was known for his talent with dice and became the youngest "bust out" man (switching crooked dice in and out of games). When the Mob shifted their gaming interests to Las Vegas, the operators of the new casinos relied on Steubenville for talented table workers.

Dino rose through the Mob ranks not as a thug, but by brains and became Jimmy "Blue Eyes" Alo's and Meyer Lansky's top lieutenant. By his sheer mathematical genius, self-discipline, charm and charisma, Cellini parlayed his overall talent to become the Mafia's preeminent casino mastermind, and a "Master Casino Operator Extraordinaire." As Lansky's highest deputy, Cellini would create the Mafia's casino haven in Havana Cuba in the 1950's. He ran the mob-backed Riviera and Tropicana Clubs in Havana. He also ran a croupier school in the Hotel Nacional. During those years, Cuba was a greater cash cow than Las Vegas. Cellini's operations would net untold millions for the Mob.

In 1959, the Cuban Revolution overthrew the Batista regime, the new Cuban president, Fidel Castro, closed all the casinos and forced the American mobsters to leave the country. When Castro came to power, Dino spent a year in a Cuban prison before he was expelled. Early in the 60's, Cellini was also briefly involved in the aborted CIA operation to assassinate Castro. After leaving Cuba, Dino Cellini along with his brother Eddie ran casinos in the Bahamas. Dino worked at the Lucayan Beach Hotel and Monte Carlo Casino for Meyer Lansky and Angelo Bruno. Dino and Joe Nesline ran croupier schools, training British Subjects to work in the Bahamian Casinos. In March of 1964, the Cellini brothers were expelled. By Bahamian law only citizens of the British Isles were allowed work in the casinos.

The Cellini brothers along with the Ayoub brothers headed to Europe to run gambling operations in Rome and London. Cellini ran a croupier school in the

United Kingdom and he helped manage the Colony Sports Club casino in London with actor George Raft. However, based on a Scotland Yard investigation, Cellini and Raft were barred from participating in legalized gambling establishments in the United Kingdom. Between Cuba, the Bahamas and Britain Dino Cellini was constantly being expelled from Island Nations.

Dino Cellini in front of George Raft's Colony Club
Jokingly imitating George Raft's publicity photo
(photo Dino Cellini's son Dino R. Cellini)

In the mid 1970s, the Cellini brothers, Joe Nesline, Charlie Tourine and the Ayoub brothers acting as part of Meyer Lansky's network began dealings in Hamburg, Germany with Wilfrid "Frieda" Schulz, the "King of Sankt Pauli," Hamburg's red-light district. Schulz owned restaurants, he was a fight manager, a thief, pimp, gambler, and extortionist. Another of Nesline's connections in Hamburg was Davoud Dargahi, an Iranian national living in Hamburg who was associated with Schulz in organizing boxing matches and various criminal activities. Iranian authorities claimed Dargahi was involved in the smuggling of heroin to the U.S. The Cellini's along with Nesline also partnered with Maurits de Vries aka "Zwarte Joop" (Black Joe, because of his black hair), the ruler of Dutch gambling who was known for his night clubs with live sex shows. The Mob's first gambling investment in the Netherlands was $1 million into Club Cabala, the first professional casino in Amsterdam which opened in 1976. They then opened another casino called Club 26. The casinos were managed by Dino and Goffredo Cellini and Fred Ayoub. They supplied casino personnel from Cuba, the Bahamas, England and Las Vegas. The casinos netted 4 to 5 million dollars a year which was split 50/50 with the Mob and their Dutch partners. The Mob left Amsterdam after the Netherlands legalized gambling with the Games of Chance Act in 1986. From that moment on the Dutch government started organizing lotteries to give their own budgets some flexibility, and there was not much left for Lansky's crew.

Dino Cellini was associated with a Washington, D.C. based public relations firm operated by Edward K. (Kiper) Moss. His brothers Edward and Goffredo and his sister Julia were also associated with the firm. Julia Cellini ran Moss's secretarial services and she was also his mistress. When the Cuban and American mobsters began their collaboration in the Havana casino, they hired Moss' public relations firm. Moss was a good choice for the job; CIA files revealed Moss had "longstanding connections" to organized crime in the United States. The files stated, "Moss's operation seems to be government contracts for the underworld and possibly surfaces Mafia money in legitimate business activities." The government contracts operation probably started during World War II. In

1962, the CIA's Office of Security decided to use Moss as a contract agent for their political warfare staff. In the 1970s, Edward Moss was the public relations agent for arms dealer Adnan Khashoggi, at the time "the richest man in the world."

30

"Big Juice"

Clifford Jones

Senator Estes Kefauver, (left) Chairman of the

Senate Committee to Investigate Crime in Interstate Commerce,

Talks with Nevada Lieutenant Governor Cliff Jones

(photo Associated Press)

In 1964, Joe Nesline along with his wife Josephine and associate/money courier Heidi Rikan took a trip to the Middle East. They stayed at the Hotel/Casino du Liban on the outskirts of Beirut, Lebanon. At the time Beirut was known as the "Paris of the Middle East." The manager of the casino was Joe's old friend Clifford Aaron "Big Juice" Jones, the former Lt. Governor of Nevada. Joe's entourage also kept company with members of the Kuwaiti royal family.

The Casino du Liban first opened in 1959 and soon the richest elite of European and Arabian societies ventured into the casino in formal black-tie attire. It hosted many French and European events such as music festivals and beauty pageants. Performers at the Casino's night club included Duke Ellington, Julio Iglesias and Lebanese/American entertainer Danny Thomas. Visitors at the casino included King Hussein of Jordan, Albert II, Prince of Monaco, the Shah of Iran, Aristotle Onassis, Omar Sharif and other notable personalities. Even the mastermind of the 9/11 terror attack on the United States Osama bin Laden frequented the Casino du Liban. Osama started life as the son of a billionaire construction magnate in Saudi Arabia with close ties to the Saudi royal family.

The two-term Democrat Lt. Governor from 1947 to 1954, Clifford Jones was known as "Big Juice" for having the clout and connections to get deals made. After leaving political office Cliff Jones was instrumental in the founding of the Bank of Las Vegas which later became Valley Bank of Nevada, one of the few banks in this time period to make loans to Nevada casinos. At various times he had been given interests in casinos by people he had helped in obtaining leases and gaming licenses, including the Pioneer Club, the El Cortez and the Algiers Hotel. He parlayed those interests into a stake in other Las Vegas Clubs; the Dunes, Golden Nugget, Thunderbird and Westerner casinos. This was the beginning of a gaming career that took him around the world.

On November 15, 1950, Lt. Governor Cliff Jones was interviewed by the Kefauver committee investigators. When asked what he thought about the fact that so many people involved in Las Vegas Casinos had criminal records, he famously responded, "I would say that I believe as long as they conduct themselves properly that I think there is probably no harm comes to it."

One of Cliff Jones' front-men in investments that earned him super profits was Robert G. (Bobby) Baker, a political advisor and Democratic Party organizer. In 1955, Baker became secretary and close friend to the U.S. Senator from Texas, Lyndon Baines Johnson (LBJ). Baker became involved in helping the Inter-continental Hotels Corporation to establish casinos in the Dominican Republic and he arranged for associates of Meyer Lansky and Sam Giancana, to become involved in the casino deal. When the first of these casinos were opened in 1955, Baker and LBJ were invited as official guests.

Bobby Baker was Lyndon Johnson's "bagman" in dealing with Jimmy Hoffa, Carlos Marcello and Dallas Cowboys owner, Clint Murchison. Murchison paid Baker to secure a government contract for a meat-packing company he owned in Haiti. In 1960 LBJ was elected as vice president under John F. Kennedy. Baker remained as Johnson's secretary and political adviser and continued to do business with Giancana and Hoffa associates. Bobby Baker became a millionaire although his government salary was only about $20,000 a year.

In 1961 Baker established the Quorum Club. This was a private Washington, D.C. club in the Carroll Arms Hotel on Capitol Hill. Its members included senators, congressmen, lobbyists, Capitol Hill staffers, and others. The all-male members began paying attention to an attractive waitress at the club, Ellen "Elly" Rometsch. In 1955, Elly and her family fled East Germany for the west. In 1961, she moved to the United States with her husband, a sergeant in the West German air force who was assigned to the German Embassy in Washington. Elly became popular at the club and met socially with many of the members. Baker introduced "Elly" to JFK at the president's request. He often arranged for women to meet politicians. Baker denied he was a pimp: "I'm not saying that nobody ever left the Quorum Club to share a bed with a temporary partner, or that certain schemes were not hatched there, but I could make the same statement of Duke Zeibert's."

Baker told LBJ about Kennedy's relationship with "Elly," and LBJ informed his friend, J. Edgar Hoover. FBI agents soon questioned Rometsch about her past. They came to the conclusion that she was probably a Soviet spy. The president's brother, U.S. Attorney General Robert Kennedy intervened. In exchange for a payoff, she agreed to sign a statement formally "denying intimacies with important people." Bobby Kennedy then contacted Hoover and asked him to persuade the Senate leadership that a Senate Rules Committee investigation of the story was "contrary to the national interest." He also warned that other leading members of Congress would be drawn into this scandal and so was "contrary to the interests of Congress, too."

In 1964, a Saratoga Springs, New York newspaper article reported former Nevada Lt. Governor Clifford Jones bought an interest in the luxurious Casino du Liban and would run the casino's gaming tables. A company headed by Jones acquired

145

60,000 shares in the $6 million Beirut casino. Jones told the press that he and a partner represented New York and Swiss interests. Jones refused to give any details about those groups. Jones had interests in gambling concessions in the Caribbean; the Lucayan Beach Hotel and Monte Carlo Casino in the Bahamas, the Aruba Caribbean Hotel, Netherlands, West Indies and Grand Antilles Casino in Port-au-Prince, Haiti.

In 1961, Meyer Lansky incorporated under British law his Bank of World Commerce Ltd. in Nassau, Bahamas. Among the bank's many stockholders was Edward Levinson, a notorious bookmaker who operated in Chicago, Detroit, Las Vegas, Miami and Newport, Kentucky. Another stockholder was Cliff "Big Juice" Jones. The Bank of World Commerce served to handle the skim from several Las Vegas casinos. It also served as a laundromat for "Syndicate" cash to flow into the bank and flow out to the United States in the form of loans for everything from homes for other mobsters to savings and Loan associations around the country. This bank along with other shadowy financial institutions which were run by Saudi Arabian arms dealers, owned the Casino du Liban.

Another manager of this world-famous Casino du Liban was Lansky's drug smuggling Corsican contact, Marcel Francisci, the head of a lucrative international gambling syndicate with lavish casinos in Paris and London as well as Beirut. Marcel Francisci was a member of the "Unione Corse," the Corsican Mafia, an Organized Crime clan that ran the "French Connection" heroin trade between France, Canada and New York City. They were allied with the American and

146

Sicilian Mafia as well as the Neapolitan Camorra. Francisci was also a French politician, he served in the General Council of the Corse du Sud (the southern half of the French Mediterranean island of Corsica). As a young man, Marcel Francisci fought in World War II and was awarded the Croix de Guerre. Following the war, he developed a business empire that included casinos. Francisci was assassinated in Paris in 1982.

31

"The Nation's Most Unusual Jazz Festival"

The Lorton Jazz Festival

Prisoners frame a swinging Quincy Jones and Frank Sinatra (left)

Ella Fitzgerald gets groovy (center),

so does Ramsey Lewis (right)

(photo Jet Magazine)

In 1955, Father Carl J. Breitfeller, a jazz enthusiast and the Catholic chaplain for prisons in the Washington D.C. metropolitan area, Lorton Prison and the Women's Reformatory at Occoquan, Virginia, started what was to become known as the Lorton Jazz Festival. The festival was arranged and staged by Father Breitfeller and his fellow Catholic Prison Chaplains. With time the annual show featured some of the biggest names in Jazz, with a captive audience of 2,000 felons serving long sentences. The press described the annual event as the

148

"Nation's most unusual jazz festival." Father Carl did not consider the festival as a coddling or pampering of prisoners but an annual reminder that the prisoners are understood and thought of as human beings. The duties of Master of Ceremonies were handled by Felix Grant of the local D.C. radio station WMAL. The artists that have performed at the festival included: Nancy Wilson, Sarah Vaughan, Louie Armstrong and his All Stars, Charlie Byrd Trio and other jazz greats.

According to Joe Nesline's wife's memoirs, Josephine Alvarez-Nesline recounts the story when Joe helped out Father Breitfeller. In the summer of 1965, Joe got a call from his friend Father Breitfeller asking for a favor. Since the priest had developed symptoms of Parkinson's disease, he asked Joe to reach out to Frank Sinatra to participate in the benefit concert for the inmates. Nesline, who was also a jazz enthusiast said he would make some calls and see what he could do. The Lorton Reformatory was a prison run by the District of Columbia Department of Corrections in Lorton, Virginia about 19 miles outside of Washington, D.C.

Joe called Jilly Rizzo in New York, Frank Sinatra's right-hand man. Joe also called a woman named Peggy Strassberg who was an intimate friend of Sinatra. Joe and wife Josephine met Ms. Strassberg when she was the hostess at Anna Maria's restaurant, a long-time dining institution located on Connecticut Avenue, N.W. Washington, D.C. Peggy Strassberg eventually went to work for the comedian Jackie Gleason on his show based in Miami, Florida. Peggy met Frank Sinatra

149

through Jackie Gleason at the Fontainebleau Hotel in Miami Beach. It was Peggy who got the message to Sinatra. Frank Sinatra responded to Joe and said he would be delighted to help with the arrangements for the Jazz festival for Father Breitfeller.

That Jazz concert at Lorton Reformatory was featured in an article from the July 29, 1965 issue of Jet Magazine's entertainment section. "At Lorton Reformatory a truly captive audience tapped the beat to Frank Sinatra's rendition of 'Luck be a lady tonight.' With Sinatra on the canopied stage on the baseball field was Quincy Jones, directing the Count Basie band with Basie himself on the piano. The tenth annual concert also highlighted Ella Fitzgerald with Tommy Flanagan's Trio and other musicians who were appearing in the Washington area at the time. All artists appeared at the festival for free and, like Ella, liked to come back from year to year to perform for an enthusiastic audience."

At the nation's most exclusive Jazz festival, the only outsiders that attended the 1965 concert besides the performers were Mia Farrow, Frank Sinatra's wife at the time, Don Hewitt the producer of the CBS 60 Minutes news program and Joe Nesline's wife Josephine Alvarez. Joe did not attend the concert within the prison walls. Father Breitfeller and Josephine met Joe at Duke Zeibert's restaurant after the concert to celebrate the success of the event.

Father Carl J. Breitfeller accepting an award from inmates

Guitarist Charlie Byrd and Master of Ceremonies Felix Grant

On stage at the Lorton Jazz Festival

(photo Washington Research Library Consortium)

The Lorton Prison at Lorton, Virginia, closed in the late 1990s. As a result of the National Capital Revitalization and Self-Government Improvement Act of 1997, sentenced D.C. felons were transferred to the Federal Bureau of Prisons.

In 2018, Lorton officially reopened as a sprawling complex of apartments called Liberty at Lorton.

Father Carl J. Breitfeller, died in December of 1991.

32

"An Extra Skim"

Manny Kimmel, "Mr. X"

During their European sojourn in the 1960s, Joe Nesline and Charlie Tourine, as Meyer Lansky's and the American Mob's emissaries, set up and managed American style gaming and casino operations in major cities of Western and Eastern Europe. While in Europe Joe Nesline started another money-making scheme when he partnered with Emmanuel "Manny" (Alabam) Kimmel, a major syndicate gambler who was banned from Las Vegas and Reno for card counting.

Joe Nesline and Manny Kimmel entered into a card counting venture at the blackjack tables of the newly organized casinos. Joe's wife Josephine and his money courier, Heidi Riken, accompanied Joe and Manny on their skimming ventures. The Europeans were not yet experienced enough with the American games. The pro gamblers were taking off huge scores. Josephine took the loot to various local banks and converted the country's currency to U.S. dollars and Heidi transported the funds back to the states. This was the only time Joe involved his wife in his schemes.

Manny Kimmel, (born 1896, died 1982), was a notable underworld figure from the 1930s into the 1960s. He was a former bookie and bootlegger from New

Jersey and later an expert card counter who was banned from American casinos. Manny Kimmel was referred to as "Mr. X" in the classic book on card counting, "Beat the Dealer" by Edward O. Thorp. "The Mathematician" Edward Oakley Thorp is an American mathematics professor, author, hedge fund manager, and blackjack player. In the late 1950s, Thorp analyzed the game of blackjack to a great extent and devised card-counting schemes. Thorp decided to test his theory in practice in Reno, Lake Tahoe, and Las Vegas using $10,000 start-up capital provided by "Mr. X," Manny Kimmel. Thorp and Kimmel first visited Reno and Lake Tahoe establishments and his theory was verified since he more than doubled their investment in a single weekend. Next, they tried their card counting method in the Las Vegas Casinos with tremendous success.

Thorp and Kimmel hid their identities using wrap-around glasses and fake beards so they would not be compromised. This was essential at the time because if anyone in the casino were to recognize them, they would be kicked out immediately or worse. After his experiment proved to be a great success, Thorp decided to put his knowledge into writing and released "Beat the Dealer," which taught amateurs how they could profit from blackjack. This book immediately became a New York Times bestseller after selling 700,000 copies.

At one time Manny Kimmel was one of the biggest sports books in the country. He founded the Kinney Parking Company which was linked to Newark, New Jersey bootlegger Abner "Longy" Zwillman and Joseph "Doc" Stacher. Manny leased his garages for liquor storage during prohibition. Mob Boss "Fat

153

Tony" Salerno laundered money from one of his sports-bookmaking fronts through Kinney. The Kinney Parking Company was a chain of parking lots and garages that eventually evolved into Kinney National Services Inc., then Warner Communications and ultimately into the Time WarnerMedia Empire.

Prior to its public listing in 1960, the Kinney company merged with a funeral home owned by Steve Ross (Steven Jay Rechnitz) which then expanded into car rentals, office cleaning firms and construction companies. Eventually Ross bought out the Kinney Parking Company. The evolution of Manny's parking garages into the media empire is documented in the book "Master of the Game": Steve Ross and the Creation of Time Warner, by Connie Bruck.

At the height of his fame, Frank Sinatra hung out with a gang of entertainers that included, Dean Martin, Sammy Davis, Jr., Joey Bishop and Peter Lawford. They called themselves the "Rat Pack." They called Sinatra "Chairman of the Board." Though it is not generally known, the title originated from the fact that Sinatra was Chairman of the Board of Reprise Records, a company he founded as his own record label.

In 1967, Jack Warner sold his stake in the Warner Bros. company to Lou Chesler's Canadian company, Seven Arts Productions. When Sinatra sold Reprise to Warner Bros–Seven Arts, Inc., he retained a 20% stock interest and veto power for any future mergers. In 1969, Steve Ross made a $400 million bid for Warner Bros.–Seven Arts. It proved to be a difficult negotiation due to Frank Sinatra's

154

stock interest in the Reprise Records subsidiary. Ross had to buy Frank Sinatra's 20% shares in Reprise Records, while keeping Frank on as it's Chairman of the Board.

Sinatra had just built a lovely home for his newly widowed mother Dolly Sinatra in his old hometown of Hoboken, New Jersey. The final negotiations took place in Dolly's new home. Frank signed the assignment form on the back of the stock certificate, transferring his 20% interest in Reprise to the new company, Warner Communications Inc. (WCI), and handed the certificate to Steve Ross. In return, Steve handed Frank a check for $22.5 million. After the deal was settled, they all celebrated with delicious cookies baked by Dolly special for the occasion. The new company "Warner Communications Inc." rapidly became a Fortune 500 company.   WarnerMedia is an American multinational mass media and entertainment conglomerate headquartered in New York City.

In the United States WarnerMedia is now one of six conglomerates that own 90% of all mass media which include movie and TV productions, News and Sports operations, cable channels, music industry, internet access, publishing and video games.

33

"The Mob Mecca"

"Playground of the Rich and Infamous"

Notorious Miami Neighbors

In the mid 1960s Joe Nesline and wife Josephine frequented their vacation home in the plush Blair House Condominiums in Miami, Florida. Joe purchased the condo on the Sans Souci Island resort for his wife on her 24th birthday. The condos were built in 1961 on the Island Resort with a $2 million loan from the Teamsters pension fund. The Neslines often partied with their infamous friends and neighbors. Among Joe's fellow residents at the Blair House were Teamster president Jimmy Hoffa, New York Genovese Boss Anthony "Fat Tony" Salerno and other underworld figures. Other neighbors that Nesline was especially close to were gamblers and "Odds Makers" Lefty Rosenthal and Gil Beckley.

Hundreds of Mafiosi at one time or another maintained a residence in the neutral territory of South Florida, mostly in Broward, Palm Beach and Miami-Dade counties. At least 15 of the nation's 25 organized-crime families were represented in the area. Today there are tours of the homes and haunts of the hoods. It first began in 1927, when the most infamous of the hoods "Al Brown" (Al Capone) wintered in Miami Beach. By 1928, Capone was living in a $150,000

Venetian Loggia. The white stucco waterfront house, located on Palm Island in Biscayne Bay, originally belonged to St. Louis brewer Clarence M. Busch. Members of the City Council opposed Capone's presence in their community. Among those casting a vote against Capone was Miami Beach mayor, J. Newton Lummus, even though it was the mayor's real-estate firm that sold Capone the Palm Island house. Months before the sale, the mayor had said, "Capone is no worse than a lot of others down here."

Poker games and parties were common at Capone's estate. Among the guests were Al Jolson, Eddie Cantor, Joe E. Lewis and other entertainers who performed in Miami nightclubs. On St. Valentine's Day in Chicago in 1929, Capone invited more than 100 people to his Palm Island home for a party. On that same day Capone's thugs murdered seven members of the rival Bugs Moran gang in Chicago. Capone's guests, provided him with plenty of witnesses who could account for his whereabouts at the time of the killings, the infamous "St. Valentine's Day Massacre."

It wasn't until after World War II, when Meyer Lansky started investing Mob money in real estate in Florida and the Caribbean that the Mob's migration to the tropical climes began. Lansky pioneered the laundering of mob money into legitimate businesses. He persuaded mob bosses to move their money into more profitable and less risky ventures such as banking and real estate. In south Florida he established jukebox distribution outlets and a chain of illegal and profitable gambling casinos. In contrast to Capone who was large, loud and flamboyant, Meyer Lansky was small and soft-spoken. Lansky lived his last years in a secluded apartment on the second floor of the 14-story Imperial House condominium and was often seen walking his little dog. Lansky had no colorful moniker such as "Scarface," most often the mob's financial genius was referred to as the "Man in the Gray Suit." In the early 1950s, the Kefauver Committee heard testimony from Broward County Sheriff Walter Clark confessing that for twenty years he had provided "special policing" for Lansky's illegal gambling houses and even deputized Lansky's men who transported cash in armored cars from the casinos to banks.

In 2012, the STARZ network created "Magic City," an American drama television series set in 1959 Miami just after the Cuban Revolution. Magic City tells the story of the owner of Miami's most glamorous hotel who is forced to make an ill-fated deal with a Jewish Mob boss to ensure the success of his glitzy establishment. In a review of Magic City in South Beach Magazine, Joseph Brown wrote; "Magic City highlights a part of Miami's history that many consider the city's most glamorous era. It was a time when Sinatra crooned in the big Miami Beach hotels while Mr. & Mrs. America took Cha-Cha lessons by the pool."

34

"Las Vegas Pioneer"

Frank Rosenthal

The first time Frank Sinatra ever appears on a Talk Show

was on the Frank Rosenthal Show at the Stardust in Las Vegas

August 27, 1977

(photo Wolf Wergin, Las Vegas News Bureau)

One of Joe Nesline's neighbors at the Sans Souci Resort Island was his associate Frank "Lefty" Rosenthal, a gambler and gangster. Lefty was arrested along with Joe and others at Joe's Club "George Raft's Rendezvous" in St. Mary's County, Maryland, when it was raided by police in 1963. When arrested Lefty gave the same address as Joe Nesline to the police.

"Lefty Rosenthal" (Norman Lawrence Rosenthal), was born in 1929 and grew up on the West Side of Chicago. Lefty learned sports betting in the bleachers of Wrigley Field and would often skip classes to attend sporting events. By the mid-1950s, he was working with the Chicago Outfit. He was chosen for his expert odds making ability. Based out of Cicero, Illinois, Lefty ran the "Cicero Home Improvement Company", one of the biggest illegal bookmaking operations in the U.S.

He managed the "Outlaw Line" for the Chicago Mob. The Outlaw Line got its name from the early days of illegal gambling. Prior to an official line being published, bookmakers would go to their professional gambler friends to gauge their response to the initial, unpublished, betting lines. The enforcer of the Outlaw Line was Lefty's childhood friend Anthony "The Ant" Spilotro, a Chicago Mafia soldier. Lefty had a long list of sports teams' personnel who received money in return for supplying him with inside information. In 1960, Lefty was charged in North Carolina with conspiring to fix a basketball game between New York University and West Virginia University during the regional finals of the NCAA tournament in Charlotte, North Carolina. He had offered a bribe to one of the NYU players to shave points and win by less than the bookies published spread. Lefty pleaded nolo contendere (no contest) in 1963 and was fined $6,000.

After being indicted as a conspirator on multiple sports bribery charges in Chicago, Lefty moved the operation to Miami. By 1961, Lefty had acquired a national reputation as a sports bettor, oddsmaker, and handicapper. Lefty was a suspect in multiple business and car bombings in the Miami area during the infamous "Bookies War" in the 1960s. The FBI opened a case file on Rosenthal and a subpoena was issued for him to appear before U.S. Senator John McClellan's subcommittee on Gambling and Organized Crime. He was accused of match fixing but was never charged. He invoked the Fifth Amendment 38 times. Due to this, he was barred from racing establishments in Florida. In order to escape police attention, Lefty moved to Las Vegas in 1968, followed by his friend Anthony Spilotro.

A pioneer of sports gambling, Lefty secretly ran the Stardust, Fremont, Marina, and Hacienda casinos when they were controlled by the Chicago Outfit. He created the first sports book that operated from within a casino, making the Stardust one of the world's leading centers for sports gambling. Another Rosenthal innovation was to allow female blackjack dealers, which in one year doubled the Stardust's income. Lefty hosted a television talk show sponsored by the Stardust. His first guest, not surprisingly, was Frank Sinatra.

In 1976, when authorities discovered that Rosenthal was secretly running casinos without a Nevada gaming license, they held a hearing to determine his legal ability to obtain one. The hearing was headed by Nevada Gaming Board Chairman (and future Democrat U.S. Senator) Harry Reid. Lefty was quickly denied a license

161

because of his reputation as an organized crime associate, particularly because of his friendship with Chicago mobster Anthony Spilotro. It has been alleged that the murder rate went up 70% in Las Vegas after Spilotro followed Lefty to Las Vegas. Lefty survived an October 4, 1982 assassination attempt in Las Vegas at the parking lot of Tony Roma's restaurant, in which a bomb was detonated when he started his 1981 Cadillac Eldorado. The question of who tried to blow up Lefty Rosenthal remains unanswered.

Although Sports Illustrated once crowned him as the greatest living expert on sports handicapping, "Lefty" Rosenthal eventually wound up being listed in Nevada's "Black Book" of unsavory types banned from the State's casinos because of his ties with the Mafia. "He's one of the originals," said Nick Pileggi, the author and screenwriter of "Casino." "When Lefty went down, the new Las Vegas emerged, the corporate Las Vegas." In Martin Scorsese's 1995 movie "Casino" the character Sam "Ace" Rothstein, played by Robert De Niro was inspired by Lefty Rosenthal.

35

"Layoff Operator"

Gilbert Beckley

Gilbert Lee Beckley

"Gil the Brain"

(photo Quixotic Joust)

Another associate and neighbor of Joe Nesline's at the Sans Souci Resort Island was Gil "The Brain" Beckley. In the 1940s, a national betting layoff operation was established in Newport, Kentucky under the control of Meyer Lansky and the New York Mob. The "Layoff Operators" provided a service for bookmakers by covering bets too large for the local bookies for a fee. Gil Beckley was the Mafia's top layoff bookmaker. Lower-level bookies layoff bets with other bookies like Beckley to protect themselves from big losses, in the way that insurance companies spread risk around to other companies. Gil Beckley started layoff betting in Indianapolis in the mid 1940s, moved to St. Louis, then on to Newport, Kentucky and became a national figure. Due to the heat from the Kefauver hearings in 1951, Beckley moved the operation to Canada, then back to Newport in the Glenn Hotel in 1955. In 1961, Beckley was called to testify before the McClellan Committee. He took the "Fifth" twenty-five times.

Gil Beckley was a valuable man. He helped the Mob flourish in the field of betting on college and professional athletics by handling as much as $250,000 worth of bets daily. Beckley mastered all the tricks of his trade; trolling for information from locker rooms, occasionally bribing athletes and computing odds in his head. He was known as one of the biggest sports gambler and handicapper in the United States. Throughout the 1950s and 1960s Beckley was believed to have been a major NFL game-fixer. According to FBI reports, Gil Beckley along with Charles Tourine and "Fat Tony" Salerno had over a million-dollar investment in the Miramar Hotel Casino in Antigua, British West Indies.

In January 1966, Beckley's home at the Blair House in Miami was raided by the FBI. They were looking for evidence of illegal sports betting. Simultaneous raids were executed in New York, New Orleans and Baltimore. Recovered from these raids were "Black Boxes," a device invented by Walter L. Shaw, Sr. Joe Nesline's condo was not targeted in those raids but he knew all about the "Black Boxes" and explained to his wife Josephine how these devices were used. He described how the electronic device attaches to a telephone and distorts the telephone signal, bypasses the telephone company and prevents the call from registering long distance charges. Beckley had been using these "Black Boxes" as a means of illegally transmitting wagering information.

In 1967, the Internal Revenue Service launched an investigation referenced as "National 125 Baltimore" after two games played by the Washington Redskins were taken off the betting boards in New York. The targets of the investigation were Gil Beckley's D.C. based associates including Joe Nesline, Eugene "Jabba" Corsi, David A. "Shaggs" McGowan and Richard A. "Ritchie" McCaleb. According to an IRS memorandum all were "engaged in conducting football pool wagering." The federal investigation into an NFL betting scandal involved Joe Nesline and Washington Redskins football players. In 1968, court records showed subpoenas had been issued for two Redskin players, but were withdrawn without being served. The football commissioner Pete Rozelle said all the players were innocent of any wrongdoing and court sources stressed they had been called only to give information.

Neither Nesline nor any of the Redskins players were charged. Gil Beckley and the other three defendants were convicted on conspiracy and racketeering charges and sentenced. Beckley entered into a deal with the FBI and the National Football League investigators to tip them off about point spreads, possible fixes and tampering with games. Such a double life proved to be dangerous, possibly even fatal. He forfeited a $10,000 bond by failing to appear for a trial on forgery

165

charges in Atlanta, Georgia. He disappeared without a trace in 1970 and his body has never been found. Beckley was declared dead in 1977.

According to Dan Moldea author of "Interference, How Organized Crime Influences Professional Football," the last person to see Beckley alive was an Atlanta-based member of Beckley's national bookmaking syndicate by the name of Elmer Dudley. Dudley claims that Beckley decided to flee the country to escape prison, and that Beckley had asked Dudley to drive him to the airport in Montreal, Canada. "He had a suitcase with over a million dollars in it." After dropping Beckley off in Montreal, Dudley never saw Beckley again. Federal law enforcement sources believe the Patriarca Crime Family of New England was responsible for Beckley's disappearance. Other sources believe that New York mobster "Fat Tony" Salerno, was responsible. Salerno was Beckley's banker and partner in his nationwide bookmaking operation.

36

"The Black Box"

Walter L. Shaw Sr.

Walter L. Shaw testifying before U.S. Senate
Permanent Subcommittee on Investigations
(AP photo)

Walter L. Shaw was an inventor and an American tele-communications engineer of Italian descent. His inventions include: the speakerphone, call forwarding, conference calling and the answering machine. In 1954, he was asked by President Dwight D. Eisenhower to create the Moscow to Washington hotline, the "Red Phone" connecting the two superpowers. When his bosses at AT&T repeatedly tried to get him to sign over the rights to his inventions and patents, he refused and quit after 14 years on the job. Since his former employer enjoyed a telephone monopoly in the United States, he was unsuccessful in reaping any rewards from his inventions. Desperate for money, he became involved with the Mafia. He devised a "Black Box" to make free, untraceable long distance telephone calls, which was a boon for bookmaking and other criminal activities.

In 1961, Shaw was called to Washington, D.C. to testify before United States Senate Permanent Subcommittee on Investigations, chaired by Robert F. Kennedy. He was called again to testify before the committee in 1971. Shaw told the Subcommittee members that he created the device used by gamblers to evade police wiretaps and cheat telephone companies on long distance tolls. He was arrested in 1975 and convicted the following year on eight counts of "illegal phone usage".

Walter L. Shaw's 12-year-old son Walter T. Shaw watched in anger as his father was convicted. The young Walter was comforted by an unlikely figure: New York Mob boss Carlo Gambino. He whispered to Walter Jr., "The only difference between us and these politicians, judges and senators, is they have a license to steal and we don't need one." The younger Walter became embittered by the treatment accorded his father. He left home at the age of 16 and became a prolific jewel thief. Walter and his gang, the "Dinnertime Burglars," were credited with over 2000 robberies from New York to Florida. The younger Shaw's take was in the millions. In 1978, he became a recognized soldier in the Lucchese New York Mafia family. Among his alleged victims were entertainer "Liberace," and the

168

DuPont and the Firestone families. Walter T. Shaw was eventually arrested and spent 11 years in prison.

In 2008, Walter T. Shaw self-published a memoir, "A License To Steal." The book chronicles the saga of his father, one of the most important inventors of his time, who was ripped off by corporate America. "My dad changed our lives. When he came into this world, we had rotary phones and human operators. Now we have conference calls and touch tone dialing." The actor Frank Vincent wrote in the foreword of the book, "Full of love, fear, violence, hate and the quest for redemption, this book is an unbelievable journey through life." The son also produced a documentary about his father "Genius On Hold," narrated by actor Frank Langella.

Father and son were estranged from each other for 25 years because of the son's life of crime. They reconciled and Walter L. Shaw eventually went to live with his son in Florida. The younger Shaw stated, "My wife brought him to me on my 48th birthday." Walter L. Shaw died of prostate cancer on July 21, 1996, in Fort Lauderdale, Florida. Shaw received posthumous recognition for his accomplishments from the Florida House of Representatives in 2000. Walter L. Shaw's "Black Box" was the inspiration for the "Blue Box" designed and built by Steve Wozniak. The original Black Box was analog, the Blue Box was digital. The newer device was used by the young Wozniak and Steve Jobs to game the telephone system, make free phone calls anywhere in the world and a host of other highly illegal practices. The inventive pair sold the device to their friends for $170. The fun and games ended when their enterprise came to the attention of the police and the business was shut down. The Blue Box is currently residing in the Computer History Museum in Mountain View California.

"If it hadn't been for the "Blue Boxes,"
there wouldn't have been an Apple"
Steve Jobs

"If it hadn't been for Walter L. Shaw and the "Black Box"
there wouldn't have been a "Blue Box."
Author's opinion

37

"Hanging Out with the Heavyweights"

Party at the Eden Roc Hotel

In her memoir, Josephine Alverez recounted attending a party with Joe Nesline in February 1965 at the Mob associated Eden Roc Hotel in Miami Beach. The party was hosted by Frank Sinatra and comedian Joe E. Lewis. Nesline and wife Josephine were hobnobbing with some of the Mob heavyweights. Among the guests in attendance were Vincent "Jimmy Blue Eyes" Alo, Joseph Fischetti, Anthony "Fat Tony" Salerno and Santo Trafficante Jr.

It was no secret that mobsters and their associates had a penchant for the luxury hotel business in the Miami Beach area. It was estimated that at least 40 of Miami Beach's hotels had varying degrees of Mob interest. In the early 1970s, the Justice Department set up two Strike Forces, one in Miami the other in Washington, D.C., to investigate the Mob's investments in luxury hotels and other enterprises. The investigators consisted of Mafia experts as well as tax and securities specialists. These experts were looking into highly complex securities crimes, real estate fraud and corporate swindling. At the time, the fabulous Eden Roc Hotel was owned by partners Sam Cohen and Morris Lansburgh. A federal grand jury indicted the two famous hoteliers along with Meyer Lansky for conspiring to conceal and distribute about $36 million in unreported income from hotel casinos on the Las Vegas Strip. Cohen and Lansburgh were convicted and served one year in prison. Meyer Lansky was never convicted.

Despite the Federal Strike Forces and the seemingly persistent bipartisan opposition to Organized Crime, both the Democratic and Republican Parties' 1972 National Presidential Conventions were held in the neutral territory of Miami. The conventions were held one month apart at the Eden Roc and Deauville hotels. The press credentials were issued at the Eden Roc. Both political Parties partied hardy at the Mob controlled Miami Beach Hotels.

In the 1970s, the Mafia families were attracted to the South Florida area by the narcotics trade. The Fed's crackdown on the "French Connection" drug trade between Marseilles, France, Montreal, Canada and New York City caused the drug traffickers to switch their routes through the Caribbean with Miami becoming the focal point and giving rise to the Columbian Cartels. With the law enforcement crackdown on the "Caribbean Connection" starting in the 1980s, the drug traffickers switched again to a land route, giving rise to the Mexican Cartels.

38

From Crooner to "Chairman of the Board"

Frank Sinatra

Francis Albert Sinatra

(photo Hoboken Historical Museum)

Eden Roc party host Francis Albert Sinatra, "Old Blue Eyes" was born in 1915 and raised in Hoboken, New Jersey. At birth Sinatra weighed 13 pounds and had to be delivered with forceps which left his face permanently scarred. Sinatra was always careful not to be photographed on his left side. Sinatra's father, Saverio Antonio Martino "Marty" Sinatra was an ex-prizefighter, bar owner and Hoboken City fireman. His mother Natalina Maria Vittoria "Dolly" Garavaneta, was active in Hoboken's democratic political machine. She was also a midwife and was present at the birth of some future underworld figures. Sinatra's Godfather was

New Jersey mobster Willie Morretti. In the time and place Sinatra grew up in and to the people he grew up with, friendships and loyalties were sacrosanct. Just like George Raft, Sinatra never repudiated or disassociated himself from the people he grew up with. Much has been written and speculated about Sinatra's Mob connections, most of which are in the public domain including FBI reports.

Frank Sinatra began singing professionally as a teenager. He learned music by ear and never learned to read music. He got his first break in 1935 when his mother persuaded a local singing group, the Three Flashes, to let him join. Fred Tamburro, the group's baritone took Sinatra on because he had a car and could chauffeur the group around. With the young crooner the group became known as the Hoboken Four. The group won first prize on the Major Bowes Amateur Hour Show and received a six-month contract to perform on stage and radio across the United States. Sinatra quickly became the group's lead singer and garnered most of the female attention. Due to the success of the group, Edward Bowes kept asking them to return, disguised under different names, including "The Seacaucus Cockamamies" and "The Bayonne Bacalas".

Soon after Frank Sinatra's death in May of 1998, at least 30 news organizations filed a Freedom of Information Act request for Sinatra's FBI files which were released in December 1998. The files, taken together, form a peculiarly American time capsule from World War II to the end of the 20th century. Based on the release of Sinatra's FBI file, an article appeared in the Washington Post magazine in March of 1999, titled AKA FRANK SINATRA. The article written by Jeff Leen starts;

"It Began With A Sound."

On August 13, 1943, a letter from San Jose arrived in Washington. The letter writer, whose identity remains a government secret, was worried about a sound that had come over the radio.

"Dear Sir:
The other day I turned on a Frank Sinatra program and I noted the shrill whistling sound, created supposedly by a bunch of girls cheering. Last night as I heard Lucky Strike produce more of this same hysteria I thought: how easy it would be for certain-minded manufacturers to create another Hitler here in America through the influence of mass-hysteria! I believe that those who are using this shrill whistling sound are aware that it is similar to that which produced Hitler. That they intend to get a Hitler in by first planting in the minds of the people that men like Frank Sinatra are O.K. therefore this future Hitler will be O.K."

On September 2, the letter writer received a reply:

"I have carefully noted the content of your letter and wish to thank you for volunteering your comments and observations in this regard."

It was signed, "Sincerely yours, John Edgar Hoover, Director."

The FBI director's response was not merely a polite bow to wartime hysteria. His bureau used the letter about a bunch of girls cheering to open file #62-83219 "for the purpose of filing miscellaneous information" on a subject the bureau would refer to over the next 40 years as "Francis Albert Sinatra, aka Frank Sinatra."

The files tell the story of a man who, in the 1940s, appeared to Hoover as a triple threat, a growing menace socially, politically and legally. Sinatra was a crooner who socialized among the criminal elite, he was corrupting America's youth, specifically the female "bobby-soxers" and he was a "fellow traveler," code word for communist sympathizer, who crusaded for racial tolerance. In the words of journalist Pete Hamill, Sinatra would become, "the most investigated American performer since John Wilkes Booth." Although the Fed's concerns over Sinatra's influence over bobby-soxers faded by the 1950s, its obsession with communists and the Mob remained. The FBI could never prove anything criminal against him and Sinatra could never remove the stain of guilt by association.

Sinatra's talent, ambition, success and legendary status were his alone, with possible exception of a kickstart from his mother and Godfather, Willie Moretti. This was evident in the December 2015 televised special "Sinatra 100: An All-Star Grammy Concert." Broadcast from the Wynn Las Vegas' Encore Theatre the two hour CBS special celebrated Sinatra's 100th birthday. Grammy winners honoring Sinatra included, Alicia Keys, Lady Gaga, Celine Dion, Harry

Connick Jr., John Legend, Adam Levine and Usher. The show proved that the timeless "Chairman of the Board" style can be sung by anyone. Country crooners singing Sinatra included, Garth Brooks, Zac Brown and Carrie Underwood. Neil Portnow, president/CEO of The Recording Academy stated, "Frank Sinatra is a voice for all generations. His showmanship and artistry have remained unmatched since he began performing professionally in the 1930s to his recordings 21 years ago. Today he continues to gain popularity for his classic sound and signature style. It's only fitting that we join the global celebration in honor of his 100th birthday."

Sinatra recorded his first number-one hit song, "I'll Never Smile Again," in 1940. Dubbed "Ol' Blue Eyes" by his fans, Sinatra's velvety voice made 1940s bobby-soxers swoon. Soon, Sinatra had contracts with Columbia Records, R.K.O. Films, and the Hit Parade radio program. He became one of only a few performers with record sales of over 500 million. Sinatra appeared in 58 films, including both musicals and serious dramas. In 1953, he won an Academy Award as best supporting actor for his role as "Maggio" in "From Here to Eternity." The nine-time Grammy winner died in 1998 at the age of 82. In 2008, The United States Postal Service honored Frank Sinatra with a first-class postage stamp.

"He Did It His Way"

39

"The Joker is wild"

Joe E. Lewis

The long-time friends, Frank Sinatra and comedian Joe E. Lewis

Performed a two-week stand at the Eden Roc Hotel

During the first two weeks of February 1965

(Miami Archives)

Co-hosting the Eden Roc party with Sinatra was his longtime friend Joe E. Lewis (Joseph Klewan). Lewis was a nightclub comedian and singer whose career took off in the twenties. He appeared in nightclubs in Chicago, one of which was the Green Mill Gardens, a popular Southside speakeasy on the Chicago Jazz circuit. One of the silent partners in the club was Al Capone's favorite henchman, Jack "Machinegun" McGurn,. After fulfilling his performance contract at the Green Mill, Lewis was offered a sweeter deal at the New Rendez-Vous Café which was

178

run by a rival Northside gang. Lewis was warned by McGurn that if he took the deal, he would never live to open at the Rendez-Vous.

On November 2nd, 1927, Lewis played to a packed house on opening night at the Rendez-Vous and ridiculed McGurn as part of his act. One-week later Lewis heard a knock at his hotel room door. Three thugs pushed into his room and brutally pistol whipped him. One of them took out a long hunting knife and proceeded to carve his face, even taking a piece of his tongue. The thugs left him for dead, but amazingly, Lewis later crawled into the hallway where he was found and an ambulance was called.

The Rendez-Vous Cafe kept updates in the window about Lewis' condition while he was recovering at the hospital. Capone was fond of Lewis and provided him with $10,000 in order to help in his recovery. It took Lewis a couple of years to learn how to speak and regain his confidence. No one was ever arrested for the crime, since Lewis never named McGurn to the police. Lewis returned to his entertainment career as a stand-up comic. He flourished in the 40's performing USO shows during World War II. In the 1950s and 60's he was a regular performer in Las Vegas and hung out with Sinatra and other entertainers. Lewis mentioned many years later that it was Jack McGurn who indeed attacked him in 1927. The other two thugs were Sam "Momo" Giancana and Leonard "Needles" Gianola.

In the mid 1930s, McGurn was summoned to the neutral city of Washington, D.C. to stand trial by a jury of his Mob peers at the Shoreham Hotel. The trial was presided by "Lucky Luciano." Due to his irresponsible drunken behavior and his destructive temper, he was abandoned by the "Commission" and the Chicago Outfit he served. "Machine Gun Jack McGurn" was gunned down in a Chicago bowling alley on February 15th 1936, the day after St. Valentine's Day. A Valentine's Day card was left by McGurn's body which read;

"You've lost your job; you've lost your dough.

Your jewels and cars and handsome houses.

But things could still be worse you know...

At least you haven't lost your trousers."

The Green Mill Club is the oldest continuing jazz club in the country and is still operating today. There is a large wooden mural above the bar with an inscription that reads:

"Big Al was ingesting spaghetti,

Machine Gun McGurn strangely still,

Told Joe E. 'You'll look like confetti,

If you try to quit The Green Mill.'"

Frank Sinatra portrayed Lewis in the 1957 film "The Joker is Wild," based on the 1955 biography of Joe E. Lewis. In 1961, Sinatra signed Lewis to record for his label, Reprise Records. The result, "It Is Now Post Time" is one of the first LPs released by Reprise, and one of the few recorded examples of Lewis at work as a stand-up comedian.

In 1966, while performing at the Sands in Las Vegas celebrating his 50th birthday, Sinatra commented;

> "I would have the body of a 22-year-old man,
> if I hadn't spent all those years drinking with Joe E. Lewis."

40

"Partner and Protector"

Vincent Alo

Vincent "Jimmy Blue Eyes" Alo

(photo The Mob Museum)

Vincent "Jimmy Blue Eyes" Alo was one of the biggest gangsters you never heard of and a guest at Frank Sinatra's 1965 party at the Eden Roc along with Nesline and his wife. Vincent Alo was a member of the New York Genovese Crime family and was Meyer Lansky's partner and protector. Together they set up casino operations in Florida, Cuba and London. Alo was one of the hidden owners of Caesars Palace in Las Vegas and participated in the Illegal skimming operations in the casino.

Vincent Alo, born in 1904, actually tried honest work in his early life. He was on Wall Street for 5 years, but realized since his last name ended in a vowel, there would be no ascension for him in that career. So that was the last honest job Vincent ever had. He quickly took advantage of his Mob ties (his Godfather was Carlo Gambino), and started a new career as a "knock-around guy." One of his first capers, a robbery, got him sent to prison in upstate New York for 5 years. By the time he got out, it was the height of prohibition and Vincent was eager to cash in. He rubbed shoulders and worked with all the "Original Gangsters" like "Lucky" Luciano.

Once Luciano moved up to boss, he had a special job for Vincent Alo. Meyer Lansky was the Mob's money man and his well-being was of high concern to the bosses. It was now up to "Jimmy Blue Eyes" to make sure "nobody f--ked with the Jew from Miami." Alo was much more than a bodyguard. He and Meyer became inseparable as business partners and friends. They had many rackets together, from hotels in Florida, casinos in Cuba and interests in Vegas. At one time, the Chicago Outfit made a move on Meyer's Vegas casino. Since Alo was a "Made Guy", he had to have "sit downs" for over a year. It was finally settled with Meyer giving Chicago a percentage of his action. Alo remained loyal to his friend even after Meyer Lansky died. Meyer had a disabled son whom he left money to for medical needs. When Alo found out that Lansky's daughter blew all that money, he confronted her, "If I had a gun, I'd kill you right now," the octogenarian coldly told her.

"Jimmy Blue Eyes" died in 2001, at 97. The fact that his passing went unnoticed reinforced the fact that Vincent "Jimmy Blue Eyes" Alo was very good at his job. In the 1974 movie, "Godfather II", Dominic Chianese of the HBO series "The Sopranos" portrayed a character "Johnny Ola" based on Vincent Alo.

41

"A Mobster's Mobster"

Anthony Salerno

Anthony "Fat Tony" Salerno

During the Commission Trial

(photo Cosa Nostra History)

The heaviest of the mob heavyweight guests at Sinatra's Eden Roc Hotel party was Anthony "Fat Tony" Salerno, a New York mobster with the Genovese Family. Salerno was the epitome of a perfect Mobster. He spent his entire life hustling and controlling the streets of East Harlem. Sticking to the code of avoiding drug sales, he dodged the heroin bullet that brought down many of his peers. Steeped in the earliest traditions of the Mafia in the New World, he stuck to his oaths and did what he was told; his ultimate allegiance to La Cosa Nostra (This Thing of Ours) was shown when he was sentenced to 100 years in the infamous "Mafia Commission" trial in the mid 1980s.

There are no books about Salerno's life, but that's the way it should be. The Mafia originated as a "secret society," even though it has been covered almost on a daily basis by nearly every major newspaper in the world. Salerno was born in 1911, and raised in what was a large Italian enclave in Manhattan's East Harlem. As a teenager he worked for Luciano's rackets. When the Luciano family became the Genovese family, Salerno was assigned to the 116th Street Crew, and for the next forty years Salerno climbed the family ranks by controlling the lucrative Harlem numbers racket, gambling, loan-sharking, and union corruption. He never strayed far from the community, maintaining his headquarters at the Palma Boys Social Club on 116th Street. By the 1960s, Salerno ran Harlem's biggest numbers racket, with estimated earnings of $50 million a year. He served as the "front" boss of the Genovese clan, actually tricking the Feds into believing he was the boss. The real boss, Vincent "The Chin" Gigante, was happy being in the shadow, limping around in his bathrobe.

In 1959, Salerno was already well known to the Manhattan District Attorney's Office as a mobster. An investigation into the Mafia's involvement in promoting boxing found that Salerno was a secret financial backer of the heavyweight title fight at Yankee Stadium between Swedish boxer Ingmar "The Great White Hope" Johansson and the champion Floyd Patterson. The fight generated over a million dollars in closed-circuit television fees, making it the most profitable boxing match in history up to that point. The fight ended in a shocking upset when 4-1 underdog Johansson knocked out Patterson and took his championship belt. Rumors of Salerno's involvement caused a stir, but no charges were filed against him.

Salerno was one of the most powerful and wealthiest gangsters in America, with earnings in the tens of millions from loan sharking, profit skimming at Nevada casinos and charging a "Mafia tax" on New York City construction projects. In 1986, after the "Commission Case" trial, Salerno and seven other defendants were convicted of operating the "Commission" that ruled the Mafia throughout the United States. The convictions put away most of the legendary New York bosses. The Mafia Commission Trial (United States v. Anthony Salerno, et al), a criminal trial in New York City, lasted from February 1985, until November 1986. New York's "Five Families," were indicted by United States Attorney Rudolph Giuliani under the RICO Act on charges including extortion, labor racketeering, and murder.

Not long after being sentenced to 100 years in prison, Salerno penned this letter to a journalist:

"I am familiar with the foibles of RICO. It is a congressional enactment that is a prime example of the seldom used term juxtaposition incongruity. It is a plaything for frustrated drama actors such as U.S. Attorney Giuliani and his stand-in Assistant Chertoff. For actors they are, the jury box, the audience for their courtroom histrionics. For what else can it be called when a 76-year-old man who has never been convicted of anything but a tax violation is portrayed as a murderer and worse and receives a 100-year term for RICO extortion.

What is a 100 years sentence to a 76-year-old man? A death sentence, even though the Constitution of this country allegedly forbids such a sentence for a non-capital offence. When this government has (under the guise of RICO) placed all the bad guys of Italian extraction in prison, who will be next?

History repeatedly shows us that a government that relies on unprincipled abuses of authority and dubious laws has a tendency to snowball into worse scenarios. The same jurors who most shamefully allowed these RICO convictions may one day find themselves at the defendants table for nothing more sinister than belonging to the Palma Boys Social Club or the White Plains Civic Ladies Sewing Club.

Sincerely, Anthony Salerno."

On a wiretap at a mob hangout, Federal agents once recorded Salerno bemoaning a disrespectful young gangster who had called him "Fat Tony" to his face. "If it wasn't for me, there wouldn't be no Mob left," Salerno said. "I made all the guys." Salerno, who had been in failing health since entering the prison system in 1989, died of complications from a stroke in 1992.

42

"The King of Cuba"

Santo Trafficante Jr.

Santo Trafficante Jr.

at his Sans Souci Hotel in Havana, Cuba

(photo Tampa Bay Times)

Perhaps the most powerful mobster to attend Frank Sinatra's Eden Roc party with Joe Nesline was Santo Trafficante Jr. Santo was the Boss of the Tampa, Florida Crime Family. Don Santo controlled organized crime operations in Florida and was the most powerful crime lord in Batista-era Cuba. In November 1957, Santo opened the Hotel Capri in Havana and had the actor George Raft as the public face of the hotel's club. The hotel's casino was run by Joe Nesline and his overseer Charlie Tourine.

The relationship with the Trafficante family and Cuban racketeers started with Santo Trafficante Sr. during the Prohibition Era and continued with the heroin trade between Marseille, France to the transshipment point in Cuba on to Tampa and beyond. The Trafficantes, both father and son in addition to speaking their own Sicilian/Italian were also fluent in Spanish. There was a mutual respect between the Trafficantes and the Cuban American crime syndicate they dealt with, especially with the bolita lotteries in Tampa's Ybor City. The Trafficante family was credited with creating the sub-language known in the old days as "Tampan," which was of an Italian/Spanish dialect. It was spoken by the Italian/Cuban underworld element of South Florida. The dialect was used mainly to confuse law enforcement.

The Florida rackets had previously been controlled by Santo Trafficante Sr. who died in 1954. Within two years of inheriting his father's criminal organization, Santo Jr. turned it into a multi-billion-dollar international organized crime empire involving illegal gambling, loan sharking, prostitution, pornography, bookmaking, numbers rackets, arms trafficking and drugs. He also associated with the Corsican syndicate in Southeast Asia in the heroin trade. As Boss of the Tampa based crime family, Santo controlled almost the entire State of Florida, except for Miami which he shared with the top bosses of the Five Families of New York and the Chicago Outfit. Trafficante Jr. maintained relationships with almost every Mafia Family in the United States. He was most closely allied with Chicago boss Sam Giancana, and New Orleans boss Carlos Marcello. As one of the wealthiest and most powerful Mafia factions in North America, the Trafficantes were invited to represent Tampa at the 1946 Havana Conference hosted by Lucky Luciano and Meyer Lansky.

Trafficante was arrested frequently throughout the 1950s on various charges. He escaped conviction all but once, receiving a five-year sentence in 1954 for bribery, but his conviction was overturned by the Florida Supreme Court before he entered prison. Trafficante was arrested, along with other mobsters, at the 1957 Apalachin Mafia summit in upstate New York. Charges were later dropped. Treasury Department documents indicated Trafficante's legitimate business interests included several legal casinos and hotels in Cuba; a Havana drive-in movie theater; and several restaurants and bars in Tampa. He was part of a Mafia syndicate which owned many other Cuban hotels, race tracks, night clubs, restaurants and casinos. After the Castro regime seized power in Cuba, it seized foreign assets. Trafficante was arrested and incarcerated in Cuba, and his significant holdings in Cuban resorts/gaming houses, including the Capri Hotel & Casino were among the assets seized. Trafficante was then expelled from the country as an "undesirable alien." He died in 1987 in Houston, Texas.

43

"Mr. Fisher"

Joseph Fischetti

Frank Sinatra with Joe Fischetti

At the Habanero Bar in Havana, Cuba

(Early 1950s)

Lastly, another party attendee with Joe Nesline and his wife at the Eden Roc Hotel was Joseph "Joe Fish" Fischetti, the youngest of the five Fischetti brothers from Brooklyn and a cousin of Al Capone. Joe Fischetti started his career in the Chicago Outfit as Capone's chauffer. Joe Fischetti usually acted as Frank Sinatra's chaperone and bodyguard whenever Sinatra attended social functions that had a Mob connection. According to a 1962 FBI report, Joe Fischetti had the exclusive bookmaking concession at the Eden Roc Hotel. He also got a kickback from Eden Roc as a talent agent for all the entertainers performing at the hotel's club.

192

Joseph Fischetti aka "Joe Fisher" kept a promise made by his cousin "Scarface" Al Capone. He paid a visit to "Rose Marie Mazzetta" while at Frank Costello's club in New York City, the Copacabana. Most people remember Rose Marie as "Sally Rogers" on TV's The Dick Van Dyke Show in the 1960s, but she was already a pro from the age of five. "Baby Rose Marie," was a radio star for NBC, and a vaudeville entertainer. She worked on stage with legends such as George Burns, Gracie Allen, Milton Berle and other stars of the 1920s and 1930s.

In 2017 writer Marcy Knight penned an article for the Mob Museum titled "Memories of the Mob: With Rose Marie." The article starts, "Even hardened gangsters had a soft spot for an adorable little girl." Rose Marie found that to be true with the notorious Al Capone and Joe Fischetti. In the article Rose Marie reminisced about meeting Al Capone as a child performer. Her father, Frank "Happy" Mazzetta, had once worked for Al Capone. Rose Marie describes how she met "Uncle Al" Capone while working at the Palace Theatre in Chicago in 1931. The following is an excerpt of Rose Marie's recollections:

"When we got to the Palace Theatre, the doorman said to me, there's a man who wants to see your father. My father and I walked out into the alley, and there was a big man standing by a limousine. He said to my father, Hello, 'Happy.' The boys want to meet the kid. They love her, and they want to meet her. I'll have the limo come pick her up tomorrow."

"We went up the steps, into the house, and walked into a room. It had a long table in it. There were 24 guys sitting around it. I looked at them, and I looked at my father, and then I watched as Al Capone came over to me and my father. He said, Hi, Happy."

"Then Al Capone smiled, picked me up, and he said, Hello, little lady. He said, we all love you. The boys want to meet you. All of the boys stood up, and they waved to me, and I waved back. He held me in his arms, and he gave me a dinner ring. At that time, they were very popular. This dinner ring had three diamonds in it. He said, this is for you, honey. He said, Good luck with it. I want you to wear it. I said, Thank you. He said, You call me Uncle Al. I said, Sure, Uncle Al. You got it."

"While he was still holding me in his arms, he said. The guys love you, and we're going to take care of you. Don't worry about anything. If you need anything, you want anything, you let us know. We'll take care of you. He told my father, from now on, don't worry about anything. She'll be all right. We'll watch her. We'll take care of her. My father said, Thank you. I said, Thank you. He was so nice. And then he said, as he smiled, Don't forget, call me Uncle Al!"

Even though Uncle Al was sent to prison a few months later on October 17, 1931, his promise that he made to Rose Marie and her father stayed true. Capone's Outfit made sure of it. Even as an adult performer, someone was always there for her. Anytime Rose Marie worked at Frank Costello's club the Copacabana in New York, Frank would come over to her table and ask, "Do you want anything to eat? You want anything to drink? Are you being treated all right? Is there anything I can do?"

Rose Marie recalled another interesting night at the Copa. While at dinner the manager came to her and said there was a Mr. Fisher in the lounge who wanted to see her. Rose Marie told the manager, "I don't know a Mr. Fisher." The manager left, but came back a minute later and told Rose Marie Mr. Fisher said, "Yes, you do." Rose Marie then agreed to meet Mr. Fisher. Mr. Fisher turned out to be Joseph "Joe Fish" Fischetti of the Chicago Outfit. Rose Marie said, "Joe, why didn't you tell me you changed your name?" Fischetti asked Rose Marie, "Do you want anything? You need anything? They treating you right? You wanna eat? I just want to see that you're all right." Joe asked Rose Marie, "Where are you going next?" She told him she wasn't working. He said, "You're going to Reno or Tahoe. These are some of the other places that we have clubs."

"They kept me working all year, because every place I went, somebody owned it. I was looked after with kid gloves. It was absolutely wonderful. They'd always ask, Where are you working next? God forbid I'd say, I don't know, because they'd say, You'll be working in Tahoe, Reno or a country club in Kentucky. I was busy working. I played the Flamingo four to five times a year."

Rose Marie knew who these "Boys" were, and their reputations. "I loved every one of them. They were wonderful to me. I was treated like a queen. They were better than my father. All of them. Including Uncle Al."

195

"Baby Rose Marie" Rose Marie Mazzetta

as Sally Rogers on the Dick Van Dyke Show

(photo Flapper Press)

Rose Marie Mazzetta died in 2017 at the age of 94 at her home in California. Rose Marie always kept the ring that Uncle Al gave her.

44

"Going Legit"

The Washington Wig Company

In the mid 1960s, Joe Nesline attempted to go into a legitimate enterprise by acquiring the assets and business of the Washington Wig Co., Inc. The company was engaged in importing hair goods and the retail sale and styling of wigs and related products and accessories. The business was a five-story department store located in the District at 1224 F Streets, N.W. In the 1960s, hair styles that defied gravity were a popular fashion trend for women. The bouffant and beehive wigs eliminated the need of the tortuous process of back combing, hair spraying and twisting tresses around huge rollers. The wig business was a flourishing enterprise.

During his European travels, Joe was in Portugal where he made contacts with wig manufacturers of human hair from Hong Kong and started purchasing their products. Nesline's enterprise was incorporated as the Domalite Corporation of Washington, D.C. doing business as the Washington Wig Company. Joe brought Gabriel "Gabby" Bobrow in to run the business hands on. Gabby was one of Joe's partners when Joe was operating his floating craps game. It was Joe's plan to eventually take the company public. Joe spoke with Charlie Tourine about his business plan. At the time Tourine was dabbling in some insider trading, he had been investing in IPOs (Initial Public Offerings) of stocks. Charlie was making an immediate profit on the stocks by selling right after the initial offering at the higher price.

In February 1969, Nesline began the process of going public with Domalite and applied for an IPO from the Securities and Exchange Commission (SEC), but in June the IPO application was denied by the SEC. Published in Issue No. 69-120 of the SECURITIES AND EXCHANGE COMMISSION News Digest was Domalite's suspension order, "The Commission asserts that there was a failure to disclose (a) the background as a professional gambler and the convictions for criminal offenses of Joseph Nesline, Domalite's president and principal stockholder and (b) the present cost price advantage of the company over certain of its competitors, the loss of which may have an adverse effect on its gross profit. Moreover, according to the order, Domalite's financial statements were certified by 1R Accountant who is not "independent", as required; the company failed to file copies of the governing instruments defining the rights of shareholders; and it failed to make proper disclosure of compensation payable to officers and directors." The Feds also believed the Wig company to be a front for illegal gambling and cocaine distribution.

45

"The Borger Banger"

Boxing Champion Bob Foster

Robert Wayne Foster

(photo Cyber Boxing Zone)

On May 24, 1968, Bob Foster beat the Nigerian Light Heavyweight champion Dick Tiger in the New Madison Square Garden in New York City. According to Joe Nesline's wife Josephine, Joe bought tickets for Frank Sinatra and Mia Farrow, his wife at the time, to attend the championship fight. The tickets were sent by way of Jilly Rizzo, Sinatra's long-time friend. Compliments of Nesline, Frank and Mia had front row seats. Nesline attended the championship fight with his lawyer Barbara Babcock. After the fight Joe and his entourage partied with the new Light Heavyweight Champion of the World at Dempsey's, New York City's famous sporting bar and restaurant. The restaurant was owned by the former Heavyweight Champion Jack Dempsey.

Robert Wayne "Bob" Foster was a Light Heavyweight boxing contender from Borger, Texas by way of Albuquerque, New Mexico. He started boxing in inter-service competition while in the U.S Air Force. After discharge he went professional while living in Washington, D.C.

In a 2012 International Boxing Research Organization (IBRO) interview with writer Austin Kileen, Bob Foster told the following story; "I was not doing too good. had a black manager, Billy Edwards, who didn't know anybody and wasn't getting any good fights. I was sitting in my apartment when there was a knock on the door. When I answered it, a woman asked me if I was Bob Foster and handed me an envelope; said it was from Mr. Nesline. I opened it and there was five hundred dollars all in twenties. There was also a note from a Mr. Joe Nesline that said Merry Christmas and asked me to call him when I had the time."

"I called him and he picked me up the next morning and took me out for breakfast. Then he brought me downtown and he bought me some clothes. Then he asked what he could do for me. I said I can be light heavyweight champion of the world, because I haven't seen anybody that can fight, except for Harold Johnson. He's the best fighter I've seen out there. So Nesline called a guy named "Mushky" Salow and asked if he would like a fighter. Salow said over the phone that he didn't have anybody now, but liked that kid from Washington, D.C. by the name of Bob Foster. Nesline explained that he was standing next to him right now."

"So, the next day we drove from Washington, D.C. to Hartford, Connecticut to sign with Salow. Two lieutenants had bought my contract when I turned pro. And he had to buy them out. Salow then told Nesline to pay me six hundred a month to live off and take care of my family. Nesline then asked me what kind of car I wanted. I said I'd take a little old Cadillac. So he bought me a 1965 four door Cadillac. Then, he told me that if the FBI or anyone else asks you if you know me, just say you're a friend and that's all you know about me." So that is how I got a shot at the title."

With his daily expenses taken care of and the financial backing needed to negotiate for a title bout, Foster was free to concentrate on his career. Over the course of the next twelve months, Bob would win eight fights in a row, seven by stoppage. With Morris "Mushky" Salow putting up $100,000 dollars, there was no longer an obstacle blocking Foster's title aspirations. On May 24, 1968 Foster would finally meet Dick Tiger for the title at Madison Square Garden.

Foster's manager, "Mushky" Salow, was a well-known book-maker and loan shark who was also connected with Joe Nesline. It was an open secret that "gambling interests" had financed $100,000 to the aging Dick Tiger, which he demanded for risking his title. Those "interests" were only going to be able to recoup their outlay by betting heavily on a Foster victory. The bout had itself been initially

201

tainted by suggestions of a possible fix. This was all the more plausible because Joe Nesline and Charles Tourine had worked with Tiger on a Nigerian-based casino project.

After retiring from boxing Foster had a second career as a successful police officer and detective in Albuquerque, New Mexico. World Boxing Champ, Bob Foster died in 2015 at age 76.

Bob "The Deputy Sheriff" Foster
(photo Associated Press)

According to Adeyinka Makinde, the author of the book "Jersey Boy" (The Life and Mob Slaying of Frankie DePaula), one of Bob Foster's more controversial fights was with New Jersey light heavyweight contender Frankie DePaula. DePaula, the "Jersey Jolter," started boxing while incarcerated for breaking the jaw of a police officer's son in a street brawl. While at Rahway State Prison he met former middleweight boxing contender Rubin "Hurricane" Carter. The two became fast friends and sparring partners. DePaula claimed that he and Carter

202

once knocked out about ten other inmates in a prison brawl. After his release from prison, DePaula won the 175 lb. New York Golden Glove Title in 1962. Frankie was a strong durable fighter who had a knockout punch and could take a lot of punishment. He only trained and fought when he needed the money. He preferred being a local Jersey City hero protecting his neighborhood and friends. On October 25th 1968, Frankie DePaula fought Dick Tiger at Madison Square Garden. DePaula lost the decision to Tiger. The fight was voted "Fight of the Year" by Ring Magazine.

Suspicions that an impending bout between Bob Foster and Frankie DePaula might likely be tainted by a fix were not wide off the mark. One of the characters behind DePaula was a former New Jersey light heavyweight fighter named Anthony Gary Garafola. The controlling hand behind Garafola was a "Caporegime" within the Genovese family, James "Jimmy Nap" Napoli. Napoli was also a former light heavyweight fighter who ran one of the biggest gambling operations in the United States. He had a lot of leverage in who could appear or not appear at Madison Square Garden.

In May 1969, DePaula was arrested by federal agents along with a group including Gary Garafola and "Jimmy Nap" and charged with conspiracy, theft and possession of stolen copper. DePaula's boxing license was suspended by the New York State Athletic Commission. He was subpoenaed by the New York District Attorney's Office to appear before a grand jury investigating corruption in the boxing industry. In December of 1969, DePaula was indicted for perjury in regards to one of the responses he had given to prosecutors at the grand jury hearings earlier in the year. His codefendants were also suspected by an FBI and NYPD task force of having fixed DePaula's bout with Bob Foster.

DePaula's trial for the copper heist began on April 14, 1970 at the Federal Criminal Court in Newark, New Jersey. On May 7, the jury acquitted him of charges of possession and theft, but failed to reach a verdict on the charge of conspiracy. On May 14, 1970, Frankie De Paula was shot in an alley in Jersey City, New Jersey and died four months later. Two suspects were eventually arrested for his murder. One of the suspects was DePaula's manager Gary Garafola. Both suspects were later acquitted.

On November 10, 1989, Frankie DePaula was inducted posthumously into the New Jersey Boxing Hall of Fame.

46

"Hoodlum House Guests"

Senate Hearings on Labor Racketeering

Senator John Little McClellan

Labor Union Hearing

(photo The Fruehauf Trailer Historic Society)

From 1955 until 1973, Senator John Little McClellan of Arkansas chaired the Permanent Subcommittee on Investigations of the U.S. Senate Committee on Government Operations. McClellan conducted extensive hearings on labor racketeering. This special committee directed much of its attention to criminal influence over the International Brotherhood of Teamsters, most famously calling Teamster leader Jimmy Hoffa to testify. The McClellan Committee's investigation revealed that the Teamsters and other Unions had taken union funds for private use and discovered clear links between the Teamsters and organized crime. Hoffa faced major criminal investigations in 1957, and as a result he was arrested for allegedly trying to bribe an aide to the Select Committee. Hoffa denied the charges and was later acquitted, but the arrest triggered additional investigations and more arrests and indictments over the following weeks. One result of the probe was the expulsion of the Teamsters and two other Unions from the American Federation of Labor and Congress of Industrial Organizations (AFL-CIO). The corruption uncovered by McClellan's committee also led to the passage of the Labor-Management Reporting and Disclosure Act of 1959, guaranteeing union members that unions would be run democratically.

From 1961 through 1968, it investigated gambling and organized crime. One of the main topics of discussion at the November 1957 Apalachin, New York Mafia summit was what to do about the investigations being conducted by Senator McClellan's committee and his Chief Counsel Robert F. Kennedy. In 1963, Joseph Valachi became the committee's most significant witness. He was the first "Made" member of the Mafia to violate "Omerta", the code of silence, and testify about the history, rituals and activities of the Sicilian Mafia. Valachi named all the Bosses of the Five families of New York. During the entire run of the subcommittee, no Mafioso was ever prosecuted as a result of the hearings.

The most significant result of the subcommittee's investigations was the passage of major legislation against organized crime. The Omnibus Crime Control and Safe Streets Act of 1968, provided for the use of court-ordered electronic surveillance in the investigation of certain specified violations. The most notable legislation was the Racketeer Influenced and Corrupt Organizations statute of 1970, with the intentionally Italianate sounding acronym "RICO," which allowed organized groups to be prosecuted for all of their diverse criminal activities. These provisions helped the Feds develop cases that put almost all the major traditional Bosses in prison by the end of the 1980s.

In the early months of 1969, Joe Nesline entertained as his house guests several subpoenaed witnesses who were called to Washington to testify before the McClellan Committee. The two most notable witnesses that stayed with Nesline were Felix "Milwaukee Phil" Alderisio, Underboss for the Chicago Outfit and his bail bondsman Irwin Weiner. At that time, Nesline and his wife Josephine Alvarez were residing at the Colonnades Apartments located at 2801 New Mexico Avenue, N.W.

47

"The Outfit's Bogeyman"

Felix Alderisio

Felix Anthony "Milwaukee Phil" Alderisio
One of the Chicago Outfit's most feared "Hitmen"
(photo Chicago Mafia History)

The most notorious of Nesline's house guests subpoenaed by McClellan's Subcommittee was Felix Anthony "Milwaukee Phil" Alderisio. Alderisio's legal counsel for the hearings was Edward Bennett Williams of the high-profile Washington, D.C. law firm of Williams & Connelly. During the hearings, Alderisio refused to testify and would plead the Fifth Amendment 23 times.

Born in New York City in 1912, Alderisio moved to Chicago as a child. As a teenager, he moved to Milwaukee where he boxed under the name of "Milwaukee Phil." Alderisio began his criminal career during the Prohibition

Era. He frequently waited outside Outfit boss Al Capone's Lexington Hotel headquarters in the hope of getting a job as a messenger. In the early 1930s he began working as an enforcer. Rising steadily through the ranks during the Great Depression, Alderisio soon gained a reputation for brutality. By the end of the 1930s Alderisio was working under Jake "Greasy Thumb" Guzik, the Outfit's financial expert, as a bagman delivering payoffs to Chicago judges and police officials.

In the 1950s, Alderisio started working as an enforcer with Charles "Chuckie" Nicoletti. Their claim to infamy was a customized car, the so-called, "Hit Mobile." The black car had special switches that independently controlled the headlights and tail lights to avoid police surveillance. There was a hidden compartment in the back with clamps for shotguns, rifles, pistols and torture devices. When Alderisio wasn't killing for the Chicago Outfit he ran gambling and extortion rackets in Milwaukee. Alderisio owned several restaurants, meat packing firms, small hotels, nightclubs, bordellos and striptease joints.

In May 1962, Alderisio participated in the infamous Chicago "M&M Murders." Mobster Tony Spilotro was ordered by Chicago Outfit bosses to track down and kill Billy McCarthy and Jimmy Miraglia. The two men robbed and killed Mob associates Ron and Phil Scalvo. The Scalvo brothers were bar owners in a suburban Chicago neighborhood that was considered off limits by the Outfit. Alderisio, Charles Nicoletti, and Spilotro kidnapped McCarthy and tortured him until he gave up the whereabouts of his partner. They placed McCarthy's head in

209

a vise and tightened it until one of his eyes popped out of its socket. At that point McCarthy gave up Miraglia. McCarthy and Miraglia were later found dead with their throats cut.

Billy McCarthy and Jimmy Miraglia were part of a burglary crew headed by Spilotro's childhood friend Frank Cullotta. It was Cullotta who had to give up the names of McCarthy and Miraglia to Tony Spilotro in order to prove he had nothing to do with the killing of the Scalvo brothers. Cullotta would eventually go to Las Vegas and head Tony Spilotro's burglary ring, the "Hole in the Wall Gang."

The Chicago M&M Murders were depicted in the 1995 Martin Scorsese movie "Casino." Joe Pesci portrayed "Nicky Santoro" a character based on Tony Spilotro. Frank Vincent portrayed "Frank Marino," a composite character based on Phil Alderisio and Charles Nicoletti.

Alderisio served as an Underboss to Sam Giancana from 1967 until 1969 when he was convicted of bank fraud and extortion and sent to prison. While serving time, he died at the federal prison in Marion, Illinois in 1971 at the age of 59.

48

"Vegas / D.C. Connection"

Murder of Jerry Lisner

Frank Cullotta was a Chicago gangster with an extensive criminal record including murder on his resume. One of his murders was related to a federal extortion case in the Washington, D.C. metropolitan area.

In May 1979, five active duty and former District of Columbia Metropolitan police officers and three other men were charged in U.S. District court in Alexandria, Virginia for their roles in an elaborate, nationwide con game. Unsuspecting professional people would be told their money could be exchanged on a 3-to-1 or 4-to-1 basis for "hot" money that needed to be "laundered" by East Coast gangsters and passed onto legitimate outlets in order to mask the criminal sources. The con game ended with a phony arrest and confiscation of the victim's money by the policemen. The victims left thankful that they were not arrested. The ring preyed on doctors, wealthy professionals, successful businessmen from around the country and sometimes drug dealers. They were selected because they could afford the loss and would be reluctant to report their roles in an illicit activity. The victims were enticed to Washington for the money exchange and then swindled out of hundreds of thousands of dollars. The group had pulled off the scheme at least three or four times a year since 1975. The policemen were paid about $2,500 each per incident from the victim's money.

Alleged ring members frequently took victims to Washington's Union Station where a purported go-between would quickly show them a suitcase full of money. Often this amounted to stacks of one-dollar bills with a larger bill on top. While the "go-between" was counting the victim's money, accomplices dressed in police uniforms would suddenly appear, "arrest" the go-between and take away all the money.

The ring leader of the scheme was a Las Vegas con-man named Sherwin I. (Jerry) Lisner. Lisner was the brother-in-law of one of the former policemen. All eight were charged with a conspiracy count of bribery of public officials and inducing people to travel in interstate commerce to defraud them of more than $5,000.

In October 1979, the body of Jerry Lisner was found by his wife, shot to death in the swimming pool of his fashionable Las Vegas home. Lisner was scheduled to stand trial in U.S. District Court for the Eastern District of Virginia in the fraud scheme involving the D.C. police officers. Las Vegas police at the time believed Lisner knew about criminal activities in Las Vegas and other areas of the country and that persons unknown might have thought he was cooperating with investigations in those areas.

Tony Spilotro and Frank Cullotta were convinced Jerry Lisner was providing information to the police regarding crimes that Lisner, Spilotro and Cullotta had

212

committed. On the orders of Tony Spilotro, Cullotta shot and killed Jerry Lisner in Las Vegas, Nevada.

49

"The Outfits Bail Bondsman"

Irwin Weiner

Irwin Sidney Weiner

(photo Chicago Tribune)

Joe Nesline's other house guest subpoenaed by the McClellan committee in 1969 was Irwin Sidney Weiner, who had been "Milwaukee Phil's" and the Chicago Outfit's bail bonds-man. Weiner identified himself as the president of the Irwin Weiner-American Bonding Agency which was located across from the Chicago Police Headquarters. Weiner's agency was also the bonding company for Jimmy Hoffa's International Brotherhood of Teamsters. According to an FBI report, Weiner at one time was a Confidential Informant (CI) for the FBI's Chicago Office but his service was discontinued in 1957.

214

Each major segment of organized crime had its own bail bond connection. Weiner's American Bonding Agency was the Chicago Outfit's since 1945. Anthony "The Ant" Spilotro was a registered bail bondsman for the Cook County criminal court of Illinois. The biggest volume of bail business is directed and controlled by the criminal organization. When that organization guarantees bond for one of its members, no collateral is taken. Frequently, for hard pressed clients they have to put up collateral. This is where the bail bondsman has many possibilities of making money. The bail bondsman will demand an interest in the client's business or a share in the ownership of their real property. In a 1962 FBI report, Weiner boasted that for his services to "Milwaukee Phil" and Santo Trafficante Jr. he was given a substantial interest in the Deauville and Capri Gambling Casinos in Havana, Cuba. He lamented about substantial losses because of Castro's revolution.

After the revelations of the McClellan Committee, which investigated corruption and organized crime influence in labor unions, Congress passed Labor Management Reporting and Disclosure Act of 1959, also known as the Landrum-Griffin Act. The Bill was sponsored by Democrat Congressman Phil Landrum from Georgia and Republican Congressman Robert P. Griffin from Michigan. Other major Unions that received widespread attention from the Congressional committee besides the Teamsters, were the International Longshoreman's Association and the United Mine Workers. After passage of the Landrum-Griffin Bill, the Teamsters Union set up a program to handle the bonding requirements made mandatory by the Act. One of the bonding companies was the Irwin Weiner- American Bonding Agency.

Irwin Weiner grew up on Chicago's West Side. What he lacked in formal education he more than made up for in street smarts and a quick wit. One of his boyhood friends was Earl Ruby, the brother of Jack Ruby, the Dallas nightclub operator who fatally shot Lee Harvey Oswald, the man charged in the assassination of President John F. Kennedy. The House Select Committee on Assassinations (HSCA) in the late 1970s did an extensive computer analysis of Jack Ruby's home and business telephone numbers in 1963. Three of those calls were to Chicago bail bondsman Irwin Weiner. The HSCA feared he might have been a link for Ruby to crime bosses. Adding to suspicions, Weiner refused to cooperate with the FBI in its Warren Commission investigation of the Kennedy assassination.

Earl Ruby told journalist Gerald Posner in 1992, "I gave Irwin Weiner's number to my brother." "I had gone to school with Weiner; we graduated high school together. I used to see him on visits to California. He was a big bondsman for everyone, and he handled the Mafia. It was in the newspapers you could read about it. I thought he might be able to help Jack with the union. Jack didn't even know Weiner, for God's sake." Weiner later admitted that Ruby called him once, about his problem with the AGVA union (American Guild of Variety Artists) however, Weiner stated he did not offer Ruby any help.

Weiner gained notoriety in 1983 when two gunmen intercepted Weiner and Allen Dorfman as they walked towards a restaurant for lunch. According to Weiner, one of the killers announced a holdup and immediately began shooting. Dorfman was struck with seven bullets and fell dead. Weiner was unharmed. The Mob Bondsman's survival caused investigators to speculate that he had set Dorfman up. In testimony two months after the still unsolved murder, Mr. Weiner said he did not believe in the existence of organized crime, even though he admits he was acquainted with most of Chicago's leading mobsters. When the Chicago Crime Commission dubbed him a "soldier" in the Chicago Cosa Nostra, Weiner, half-jokingly stated he was "put out" by the low ranking.

Allen Dorfman was a consultant for the International Brotherhood of Teamsters Central States Pension Fund and an associate of the Chicago Outfit. His murder was news, but it was not a surprise. He had been a key figure in the world of organized crime for more than thirty years. Beginning with Jimmy Hoffa, successive presidents of the Teamsters had allowed him to use his position as head of the pension fund to provide sweetheart loans that bankrolled the Mafia's control of several Las Vegas casinos. The union itself, which had access to top business leaders, right up to the White House, was run as a virtual subsidiary of the American Mafia. In early 1974, Allen Dorfman, Irwin Weiner, Anthony Spilotro and others were indicted in Chicago by federal authorities for bilking $1.4 million from the Teamsters pension fund. After a witness was shot to death, allegedly on orders from Spilotro, the charges were either dropped or the defendants were acquitted.

Shortly before his murder, Dorfman had been convicted of attempting to bribe a U.S. Senator from Nevada. After his conviction in December 1982, Dorfman was released on $5 million bail pending sentencing. He stood to receive as much as fifty-five years in prison. In addition to the bribery case, the Feds were also looking into money skimming in Mob-backed Vegas casinos. "Dorfman knew the secrets of both the Teamsters and Las Vegas, if he decided to cut a deal with prosecutors in return for a more lenient sentence, many gangsters, businessmen and officials would end up in prison." The head of the Chicago Crime Commission told The New York Times, "There's no doubt in my mind that Mr. Dorfman was killed to keep him quiet ... if he ever coughed up to investigators ... this country would be shaking for a month."

Dorfman was only an associate, but his life provided a glimpse of the world of the American Mafia at its highest levels. Beginning in 1949, it took him just five years to rise from physical education instructor to millionaire, thanks to an introduction by his racketeer stepfather Paul "Red" Dorfman to Jimmy Hoffa. Paul Dorfman was the head of the Chicago Waste Handler's Union. In 1959, Congressional investigators described Allen Dorfman as the link between the Teamsters Union and the Chicago Outfit. He was indicted several times but usually managed to win acquittals. In 1972 he was convicted of conspiring to facilitate a loan from the Teamsters Pension Fund in return for a kickback of $55,000, but he served only nine months in jail. After his latest conviction, Dorfman should have been wary. The Chicago Outfit worried that a man living an affluent lifestyle would not be able to face spending a big part of that life in prison. Dorfman should have been well aware of the Mob's rule, all doubts must be resolved in favor of the organization. The Mob could not take the chance that someone like Dorfman would stay silent. Several years prior to his murder, several shots were fired in Dorfman's direction while he entered his car in Chicago. The shots were fired by "Milwaukee Phill" Alderisio. They were meant to scare Dorfman and keep him in line. This same lack of understanding may have also cost his old boss Jimmy Hoffa his life.

50

"The Disappearance of a Call Girl"

Pat Adams

In 1969, shortly after President Richard Nixon and Vice President Spiro Agnew took office, a call-girl by the name of Patricia Adams disappeared from the Capital party scene. At the time, her clients included an impressive cross section of official Washington. Metropolitan police Intelligence Detective, Carl Shoffler became convinced that the young woman had been murdered. According to Shoffler It was common knowledge in the D.C. underworld that Pat Adams had been working for a mob-run blackmail operation which for some time had been filming the call girl and her clients. Allegedly, Pat Adams threatened to blackmail the newly elected Vice President, Spiro Agnew. Agnew had been the County Executive of Baltimore County and the Governor of Maryland. For Pat, having a State official as a client was just another job, until he suddenly became Vice President of the United States.

The twenty-eight-year-old call-girl left her apartment on February 6, 1969, in the company of her boyfriend, Donald Brew. She was never seen or heard from again. Although Brew was considered a suspect in her disappearance, Pat's body was never found and her disappearance was classified as a missing persons case. With rumors of Pat Adams' blackmail attempt of Agnew, Shoffler thought it was likely that she had been murdered. The following is a quote from author Phil Stanford's book "White House Call Girl, The Real Watergate story": "When word got back to Joe Nesline, who had overall responsibility for the operation, he called in Pat's boyfriend, who happened to be a flunky in his organization. 'Your bitch is talking too much,' Nesline said. 'Get rid of her.'" Detective Shoffler could never prove Nesline's involvement in the disappearance.

In 1968 Richard Nixon selected Agnew as his vice-presidential candidate. After the election Agnew was quickly shoved aside by Nixon. Frank Sinatra helped make the snub bearable. Agnew became running and drinking buddies with Frank Sinatra, it didn't hurt that both were sons of Mediterranean immigrants from humble beginnings, and both loathed the news media. They partied hard from Palm Springs to Washington, D.C. The Sinatra compound in Rancho Mirage became Mr. Agnew's version of Mr. Nixon's retreat at San Clemente, California.

In 1972, the United States Attorney for the District of Maryland, opened an investigation of government corruption in Baltimore County, involving public officials, architects, engineering firms, and paving contractors. During the investigation it was learned that Vice President Agnew was still receiving kickbacks from his time as a Maryland official. On October 10, 1973, Agnew appeared before the federal court in Baltimore, and pleaded nolo contendere (no contest) to one felony charge of tax evasion, for the year 1967 and resigned from office. Agnew was fined $10,000 and placed on three years' unsupervised probation. His fine was paid by Frank Sinatra.

221

In 1982 Peter Malatesta, a restauranteur and former aide to Spiro Agnew published a book titled, "Party Politics- The Confessions of a Washington Party Giver." Malatesta was an intimate friend of Frank Sinatra and the nephew of Delores (DeFina) Hope the wife of legendary entertainer Bob Hope. Malatesta had been a California public relations man who came to Washington in 1969 to work on Spiro Agnew's staff as special assistant to the Vice President. When allegations of corruption against the Vice President surfaced, Malatesta gave statements to the press defending Agnew and proclaiming his boss' innocence. After Agnew plead no-contest and resigned from office, Malatesta felt betrayed and disillusioned. In his book Malatesta quotes the following conversation with Agnew soon after his resignation. The former Vice President came into Malatesta's office to thank him for his support. Malatesta interrupted Agnew and said, "What the hell did you do it for? If you're not guilty why quit? How could you do it?" Agnew said sadly, "Things happened and there are pressures that I am not at liberty to tell you about right now. I had to do what I did. Someday it will come out. You'll have to trust me." Malatesta thought Agnew's comment was ambiguous and he seemed to have more on his mind than the charge of taking kickbacks from contractors.

Upon Agnew's resignation in 1973, Malatesta pursued his real passion of becoming a "Washington Socialite." For several months he shared a house in Washington with Sinatra when the crooner was helping Agnew with his legal problems. Two years later Malatesta opened the chic private Pisces Club in

Georgetown. The club became a popular watering hole and event venue for politicos of both parties as well as Hollywood celebrities. In 1976, Peter Malatesta left the business, saying only that he had been forced out of management. Later, Mr. Malatesta wrote a weekly column about social life in Washington for United Features International, while working on his book. "I'd be shot if I told all," he once said, but he did manage to leak enough details and anecdotes to pique the public interest.

In 1974, syndicated investigative journalist Jack Anderson wrote a column on Spiro Agnew's resignation as Vice President. Former White house aides told Anderson they learned from members of Agnew's Secret Service detail that the pressure for the Vice President to resign was personal and that he did it to protect his family from embarrassing revelations. During the prosecutor's investigation, allegations surfaced that a Maryland contractor provided Agnew with a call girl in exchange for government favors. The prosecutor asserted that aspects of Agnew's personal life were ruled out of bounds. In the book "A Heartbeat Away – The Investigation and Resignation of Vice President Spiro T. Agnew," by Washington Post reporters Richard Cohen and Jules Witcover, the authors cautiously allude to spicy insights into Agnew's personal life. Agnew always claimed the allegations concerning his personal life were "laughable" and played no part in his resignation.

Pat Adam's boyfriend Donald A. Brew spent most of his life running con games and trying to evade the law. He had been in and out of jail throughout his life. For nearly 40 years, Brew had literally gotten away with murder. In 2007, while in failing health, he turned himself in to authorities and confessed to murdering his girlfriend. He confessed without implicating Joe Nesline. Although Brew said he buried her in Prince William County, Virginia, authorities were never able to find her body. The true reasons for Brew's belated confession are still unknown. He told authorities that he simply felt compelled to set the record straight. Brew, destitute and suffering from serious medical issues, simply needed a place to live, eat and receive free medical care. This led to speculation that he may have told less than the full truth.

Sitting in the Prince William County, Virginia jail, Brew calmly described to Washington Post reporters the day he killed Adams. According to Brew, he lured Adams to a wooded area near Quantico and confronted her, saying he knew that she was going to testify in an upcoming trial that he had stolen tens of thousands of dollars from the Fort McNair Officers Club and set a fire to cover his tracks. Brew then shot her in the head and buried the body. Brew was convicted of the murder. He died in a Virginia prison the following year.

In the fictionalized novel "City of Shadows" by James Dalton about the "Watergate Scandal," D.C. crime Boss "Joseph Nezneck" is responsible for the murder of "Pam Dawson", the call-girl working for his operation. According to the novel, all evidence of the murder, including the body, was destroyed by fire in an abandoned home in Prince Georges County, Maryland. While investigating the murder of Pam Dawson, fictional Washington, D.C. detective, "John Quinn," is obsessed with solving the crime and pinning it on Nezneck. During Quinn's odyssey, the detective interacts with many of the players involved in Watergate and its peripheral intrigues. Other details in the novel include the discovery of Pam Dawson's "black-book" by detective Quinn in her empty apartment. Listed in the black-book are the names; "Heidi Ryker" (Heidi Rikan, Joe Nesline's money courier), "Marjorie Bell" (Maureen Biner, Rikan's best friend and a former party-girl herself), the "Freedom Wig and Beauty Shop Inc." on F Street (Nesline owned the Washington Wig Company on F Street N.W.). Another detail in the novel is the strip club, the "Silver Moon" owned by "Joe Nezneck." Heidi Rikan started her infamous career as a stripper at the Blue Mirror Club on D.C.'s 14th Street strip.

51

"Mafia Money Courier / CIA Madam"

Heidi Rikan

Joe Nesline flanked by his wife, Josephine Alvarez (left)

and Heidi Rikan,

New Years Eve party at Billy's, a popular Mob hangout in D.C.

(photo News Spike, A Parliament of Whores-

The Sexual History of Watergate)

According to Frank Kuznik for Regardie Magazine, Joe, Josephine and Heidi were "Quite a threesome, in more ways than one."

Adelheidecharlotte Riecken had emigrated with her parents from Germany to Redding, Pennsylvania when she was 14 years old. She joined the U.S. Army and had active-duty stations in Germany and Fort Myers, Virginia, across the Potomac River from Washington, D.C. After leaving the army, the attractive blond became a nude model and a popular stripper at the Blue Mirror club along D.C.'s old 14th

226

Street N.W. corridor of strip clubs just a few blocks from the White House. Nesline had financial interests in many of the clubs along the 14th Street strip. "Heidi" Rikan, as she came to be known, eventually hooked up with Mob connected D.C. gambling boss Joe Nesline. Heidi's initial job for Joe was to become friendly with professional football players with the goal of learning the odds a football team would either win or lose. Through Joe, Heide became a money courier for the Mob between the United States, Europe and the Caribbean.

As a well-established "party girl" with D.C.'s politicos and professional athletes, Heidi Rikan became a Madam and managed a "call-girl" operation out of a 6th floor apartment at the Columbia Plaza Apartments located near the State Department and the Watergate complex. The operation had a corporate cover called "Business Services Consultants," and Heidi's business cards listed her as "Erika L. Rikan." The call-girl operation was located near the Democratic National Committee (DNC) headquarters in the Watergate at 2600 Virginia Avenue N.W. Heidi was assisted in her operation by Phillip Mackin Bailley, a court appointed defense lawyer who specialized in prostitution cases. He learned to bribe cops to not show up at the trials of the call-girls he defended. If a police officer does not show up, the case is dismissed by the judge. Heidi Rikan's association with Phillip Bailley started when she retained him to report to her on the activities of the D.C. police vice squad.

Another of Heidi's associates was the former top CIA surveillance man and Watergate burglar James McCord of McCord Associates. When employed at the CIA, McCord's division used prostitutes for sexual espionage. McCord videotaped trysts between Heidi's call girls and their clientele. To the CIA, Heidi Rikan was known as "Kathie Deiter." It is not known who was actually taped at Heidi's operation. Rikan and McCord's Columbia Plaza operation was also a focus of the so called "White House Plumbers" surveillance operation. G. Gordon Liddy, James McCord, E. Howard Hunt, along with three Cuban CIA contractors, launched a bugging operation against DNC headquarters at the Watergate. McCord and Liddy set up their surveillance nest at the nearby Howard Johnson's Hotel, across the street from the Watergate.

Peter Dale Scott, Canadian diplomat and professor of English at the University of California, Berkley and conspiracy researcher has suggested; "Washington's sex syndicate, exploited by intelligence spooks and the Mob, has driven the major scandals at least since the Cold war." In espionage terminology these sexual blackmail operations are referred to as "Honey Pots."

Heidi Rikan kept a "little-black-book" of clients which included the names and telephone numbers of Republican and Democrat politicians and government functionaries as well as athletes, mobsters, movie stars, bookies, and playboy millionaires. The athletes in Heidi's black-book were professional football players from the Washington Redskins, the Dallas Cowboys, the New Orleans Saints, the Cleveland Browns and the Green Bay Packers, as well as the team owners.

228

The government functionaries in Heidi's personal phone directory included the unlisted number of Sam Dash, chief counsel for the Watergate committee and John Dean, President Richard Nixon's aide. Heidi's little-black-book also listed Dean's girlfriend and later wife, Maureen "Mo" Dean aka "Clout" because of her connection to John Dean. Heidi Rikan and Maureen Dean were very close friends; they met in Texas when Heidi was on assignment for Joe Nesline's sports betting operation. According to a CIA draft report, Heidi and Maureen worked as strippers in Dallas and New Orleans. Most of the strip clubs in these cities were controlled by New Orleans Mob Boss Carlos Marcello. They became roommates when Maureen moved to Washington. In Maureen Dean's memoirs published in 1975, "Mo: A Woman's View of Watergate," a photograph of Heidi Rikan is included.

Maureen Elizabeth Kane was born in Los Angeles. She briefly worked as an airline stewardess and married her high school sweetheart Michael Biner a Los Angeles based stockbroker. She soon tired of both her job and her marriage. On a Dallas flight she met her future second husband George Owen, a scout for the Dallas Cowboys and the New Orleans Saints football teams and the owner of the Mob connected University Club in Dallas. George Washington Owen Jr. was an associate of sexual blackmailer Bobby Baker. Baker had once compromised President Kennedy by setting him up with a lover who was likely in contact with the Soviet embassy. It was through George Owen that Heidi Rikan met Maureen Dean. While on the Caribbean Island of Antigua working with joe Nesline, Heidi met Owen and began an affair with the notorious lothario. Through Owen's informal "Rover Boys Club," Heidi met all of the who's-who of Texas politics, sports and society.

Maureen "Mo" Elizabeth Kane-Biner-Owen-Dean would also go on to write several books. One of those books is the 1987 novel "Washington Wives." In the novel the White House Chief-of-Staff dies of a heart attack and the President must appoint a new Chief of Staff. Three beautiful, powerful women have each decided that her husband will be the one. And each will do anything to get him there. In a November 1987 article in People Magazine, writer Andrea Chambers described the book as a "steamy tale of passion on the Potomac." The novel follows the adventures of a young hot little sexpot who teams up with a more sophisticated woman named Echo Bourne. In her book Maureen Dean describes Echo as a beautiful blonde ice-maiden who controls a network of women who work for an intelligence operation that specializes in sexual blackmail for political ends. In an interview with Washington Post writer Stephanie Mansfield, Maureen Dean says "there's a little bit of me in all of the characters, including the voluptuous high-priced hooker Echo Bourne."

In April, 1972, Washington's social scene was rocked when FBI agents raided the office and home of Heidi's associate, Phillip Bailley. Coded address-books and photographs were seized, and what began as a simple violation of the Mann Act, became a grand jury investigation with ramifications throughout the Capitol. The Feds uncovered a high-priced call-girl ring headed by Bailey and staffed by secretaries and office workers from Capitol Hill and the White House. Assistant U.S. Attorney (AUSA) John Rudy was placed in charge of the investigation. The AUSA started looking into the Columbia Plaza call-girl ring and its connections to the DNC.

That same afternoon, the *Washington Star* newspaper published a front-page story, titled "Capitol Hill Call-Girl Ring." Soon a cast of future Watergate characters appeared at Rudy's office. The first was Louis J. "Lou" Russell, a former FBI agent who was forced out of the Bureau because of alcoholism. Among Russell's post-FBI gigs included security at the Watergate complex and served as a source of referrals and bouncer for Rikan's girls. He likely recorded calls from their Columbia Plaza operation for ex-CIA man James McCord's security agency, McCord Associates, on behalf of the CIA. Russell tried to divert Rudy's attention from the Columbia Plaza to another operation that serviced lawyers and judges in another part of town.

AUSA Rudy next received a telephone call from the President's counsel John Dean, ordering the prosecutor to the White House and to bring all the evidence. Rudy brought Phil Bailley's address books. John Dean wanted to check the names of the people involved, to see if any of them worked for the President. At first, Dean wanted Rudy to leave the address-books with him, but Rudy refused, pointing out that the books were entered as evidence. As a compromise, Dean's secretary was allowed to copy the books. When the secretary returned, Dean went through the copies page by page, circling the names. Bailley's address-books included the names of secretaries and wives of some of Washington's most prominent men, as well as the names of the johns they serviced. On June 9th 1972, Phil Bailley was indicted on 22 felony counts, including charges of blackmail, racketeering, procuring and pandering. Bailley was remanded to Washington, D.C.'s St. Elizabeth's Hospital to undergo psychiatric tests. Eventually, he was certified sane and plead guilty to a single felony. When he did, he was bundled off to a federal prison in Connecticut.

In the weeks following the Watergate arrests, AUSA Rudy had second thoughts. His investigation of a link between the Columbia Plaza call-girl ring and the DNC appeared to be politically-motivated. Worried about that perception, Rudy asked his boss, U.S. Attorney Harold Titus, what he should do. And the advice came back, "Chill it." The case-file, thick with interviews and evidence, was sealed and, soon afterwards was "lost." The purpose of the Watergate break-in has been up for debate and litigation for many years. Whatever its purpose, the burglary took place in the early morning hours of June 17th 1972. McCord and four of his accomplices had not been inside the DNC for more than a few minutes, when they were arrested by Metropolitan Police Detectives John Barrett, Paul Leeper and Carl Schoffler.

During interviews and depositions years later, Phillip Bailley related the following story: Bailley was having an affair with a woman he knew as "Kathie Deiter" (Heidi Rikan), a call-girl at the Columbia Plaza Apartments. She asked him to establish a liaison arrangement with the DNC. At the time Bailley was a young Democrat who liked to party. He had previously worked on the Bobby Kennedy campaign and knew a number of workers at the DNC. Bailley stated that one of those workers was Ida Maxwell "Maxie" Wells a secretary in Spencer Oliver's office. R. Spencer Oliver was the Executive Director of the Association of State Democratic Chairmen. With the secretary's help, the liaison arrangement was established.

According to Bailley, if a visitor to the DNC wanted companionship for the evening, the secretary would show him photographs she kept in her desk. According to Bailley, the photographs were in no way obscene, but were, instead, discrete pictures of attractive women. If the man was interested, he would be sent into the office of the frequently absent Spencer Oliver to await a telephone call. When the phone rang for the first time, he was not to answer it. A minute later, it would ring again and, on this occasion, he would answer it. The caller would be one of the women whose picture the visitor had seen. Knowing that the woman was a call-girl, the visitor would make whatever arrangements he pleased. Ms. Ida Maxwell Wells has always denied the allegations by Bailey. Spencer Oliver alleged he was never aware of how his phone was being used while he was gone, but AUSA John Rudy who investigated Bailley's ring, testified in court that he had evidence tying Oliver to Bailley's call-girl ring but was told by his superiors to suppress it because it was politically explosive.

Through court testimony, G. Gordon Liddy stated he was also aware of Kathie Dieter. Liddy learned Deiter's true name was Heidi Rikan, a former stripper at a

Washington nightclub called the Blue Mirror and that she was a friend of Mob associate Joe Nesline. According to Liddy the information about Heidi Rikan came from an authoritative source, Walter "Buster" Riggin. "Buster" Riggin was a sometime pimp and associate of Joe Nesline.

Whitehouse "Plumber" G. Gordon Liddy with the author

October 21, 2001

Liddy believed the burglar's objective during the Watergate break-in was to determine whether the Democrats possessed information embarrassing to John Dean. When D.C. police Detective Carl Shoffler arrested Watergate burglar and Cuban CIA contractor Eugenio Martinez, he had a desk key in his possession which he tried to get rid of. The FBI later determined the key unlocked DNC secretary "Maxie" Wells' desk. The detectives also found photographic equipment that was focused on the top of that same desk.

Some of the workings of the Nesline/Rikan Columbia Plaza operation were described in a speech by G. Gordon Liddy at James Madison University on April 2,

234

1996. In his speech, Liddy talks about a conversation with Assistant Chief of Protocol for the State Department, L. Nicholas "Nick" Ruwe. The conversation took place over drinks at Peter Malatesta's private Georgetown Pisces Club. The subject was about the high-end call girl operation, or as Nick Ruwe called it, a "Honey Trap." "We sent all the diplomats and visiting foreign dignitaries there. We knew the agency boys (CIA) were filming them." A California State politician once asked Nick Ruwe what did his job entail as chief of protocol. His response was, "We have ten Arabs coming to town, and they ordered twenty prostitutes-none of them Jewish."

After the Watergate affair with all its criminal and civil court cases, with all the journalists and authors scrambling to write the definitive Watergate story and with the cast of characters involved all trying to distance themselves from each other, Heidi Rikan was left out in the cold. Even her best friend Maureen Dean and her husband John Dean completely cut off all communications with her. After a series of failed relationships with some sugar daddies her life spiraled downward. It was reported that while drunk, Heidi tripped down a flight of stairs in her mother's home in Reading, Pennsylvania. After lingering in a hospital for several weeks Heidi died on January 27, 1990, she was 53 years old. Shortly after Heidi's death, her daughter Kathie Dickerson found her mother's personal phone directories and placed them in storage. They stayed under lock and key for twenty years until Phil Stanford published them in his book "White House Call Girl; The Real Watergate Story."

52

"The Darker Side of Heidi"

The Texas Connection

Heidi Rikan was also involved with the darker side of the Mob-CIA relationship. Heidi had interactions with a number of figures whose names were linked to the assassination investigation of President John F. Kennedy, including restauranteur and alleged Mafia associate Joseph "Egyptian Joe" Campisi, and Texas businessman Clint Murchison Jr., the principal owner of the Dallas Cowboys and son of Texas oil baron Clint Murchison Sr. Campisi was so close to Murchison, he was considered part of the Dallas Cowboys family with full access to the organization. Joseph Campisi, was the owner of Campisi's Egyptian Restaurant in Dallas. Campisi's was well known locally for its founder's connections to organized crime, a fact that the restaurant capitalized on for publicity. Campisi was associated with Joseph Civello, the head of the Carlos Marcello-controlled Dallas Mafia.

Jack Ruby, the killer of Lee Harvey Oswald, was a regular at Campisi's and was frequently seen eating there, including the night before the assassination of John F. Kennedy. After Jack Ruby's arrest for killing Oswald, Ruby requested that Joe Campisi visit him in jail. Joe Campisi and his wife visited with Jack Ruby in jail for ten minutes on November 30, 1963. While Jack Ruby was hanging out at

Campisi's, Clint Murchison, Sr., was hosting a party for J. Edgar Hoover, Richard Nixon, Vice President Lyndon Johnson and other politicos and millionaires.

J. Edgar Hoover and his FBI partner, Clyde Tolson, were regular visitors to Murchison Sr.'s Del Charro Hotel in La Jolla, California. The three men would visit the local racetrack, Del Mar. Hoover was a well-known notorious gambler. Allan Witwer, the manager of the hotel at the time, later recalled: "It came to the end of the summer and Hoover had made no attempt to pay his bill. So, I went to Murchison and asked him what he wanted me to do." Murchison told him to put it on his bill. Witwer estimates that over the next 18 summers Murchison's hospitality was worth nearly $300,000. Other visitors to the hotel included; Meyer Lansky, Johnny Roselli, Sam Giancana, Carlos Marcello and Santo Trafficante Jr.

Other interesting names in Heidi's "little-black-book" included phone numbers for Morris Jaffe, Lynden Johnson's financial adviser and for Fred Black, a close friend of LBJ. Frederick "Fred" B. Black Jr. came to Washington, D.C. as an acquaintance of Harry S. Truman. In the 1950s he became a business associate and political adviser to Lyndon B. Johnson. He was also a close friend of Mafia boss, Johnny Roselli. Fred Black was widely known in Washington as a friend of politicians in his role as a consultant for military contractors in the post-World War II arms and space races. In 1962, Black was enmeshed in a political scandal when he established the Serve-U-Corporation with his friend, Bobby Baker, and several mobsters. The corporation was to provide vending machines for

237

companies working on federally granted programs. The machines were manufactured by a company secretly owned by Sam Giancana and other mobsters based in Chicago. In 1963, a lawsuit brought by rival vending companies exposed the political corruption.

Bobby Baker was forced to leave his job as Vice President Johnson's assistant. According to Evelyn Lincoln, President Kennedy's secretary, the President had decided that because of the emerging scandal he was going to drop LBJ as his running mate in the 1964 election. In 1982, Fred Black was arrested on charges involving a scheme to launder more than $1 million in Colombian cocaine money. He was prosecuted and served seven years in prison.

53

"Another "Honey Trap" Operation"

"The Asian Gatsby"

Tongsun Park

"The Asian Gatsby"

(photo Retro Images Archives)

In the mid 1970s, Erika "Heidi" Rikan, and her Mob associate Joe Nesline, were linked to another "Honey Trap" operation run for sexual blackmail out of the George Town Club involving Korean/Taiwanese intelligence agent Tongsun Park. The rogue American CIA agent Edwin P. Wilson was a member of the club. Both Park and Wilson were listed in Heidi's "black-book." According to a federal indictment, South Korean Tongsun Park set up and operated Washington's exclusive George Town Club with the aid of Korean Central Intelligence Agency (KCIA) officials in an illegal effort to influence U.S. politicians and officials.

In 1956, Tongsun Park was a freshman at Washington's Georgetown University. After being suspended for academic deficiencies, he returned to Seoul in 1960. While back in Korea he made some powerful friends among the men closest to the South Korean president. After returning to D.C., Park acquired the premises located at 1530 Wisconsin Avenue N.W., in the exclusive Georgetown neighborhood. He leased the property in 1961 and purchased it in 1965. The George Town Club opened in the spring of 1966. During several years spent developing the property, Tongsun Park set out in search of a founding group. His hope was that the club would fly on its own with no overt link to Korea other than himself. During this time, he was also engaged in complex worldwide business dealings where he was linked to the Korean CIA as an "agent of influence". Part of the Korean influence-peddling conspiracy involved Park being designated as the seller's agent for the purchase of all rice by South Korea from the U.S. Park then used his commissions to pay off U.S. Congressmen and Senators to influence them. Tongsun Park became good friends with Vice President Spiro Agnew's personal special assistant Peter Malatesta. The "Korean Gatsby" was the main financial backer for Malatesta's private Georgetown Pisces Club.

In 1976, the influence peddling conspiracy was exposed and Park fled to London. The Club treasurer worked out a verbal agreement with Park via telephone, and the club was purchased by its members. In 1977, Tongsun Park was indicted by a U.S. District Court on thirty-six counts, to include bribery, illegal campaign contributions, mail fraud, racketeering, and failure to register as an agent of the South Korean government. The case would be known as "Koreagate." Park avoided a federal trial by testifying to the court in exchange for immunity. His testimony led to three members of Congress being reprimanded and convinced the Democrat Speaker of the House Carl Albert not to seek reelection.

Edwin P. Wilson was sponsored to join the George Town Club by former White House Cabinet Secretary Robert Gray, probably at the behest of the CIA in order to spy on KCIA Tongsun Park. Ed Wilson officially retired from the CIA in 1971 but continued to work for the spy agency as a freelancer. He ran front companies for the CIA and later built a $23 million fortune with his enterprises. In 1982, federal agents arrested Wilson. He was charged in the Southern District of Texas with selling 20 tons of C-4 plastic explosives to the Libyan government of Muammar Gaddafi. At the time, Wilson's trial was the biggest arms-dealing case in U.S. history. Wilson was convicted on multiple federal counts, and was sentenced to a total of 52 years.

Wilson worked tirelessly to disprove allegations he was a traitor. His appeal of the Texas case produced CIA records indicating he had worked for the agency on at least 40 occasions. Several of the documents showed the agency knew Wilson was working in Libya and requested his help in obtaining information. The Houston-based U.S. District Court Judge found that U.S. Justice Department prosecutors knew Wilson had worked for the CIA but introduced a false affidavit from a top official with the agency who avowed the CIA never asked Wilson "to perform or provide any services, directly or indirectly." The judge wrote in a 2003

241

opinion that "With their knowledge of the nature of Wilson's work for the CIA, they (prosecutors) deliberately deceived the court." Wilson was released from prison the following year.

To Quote the 1960s TV show "Mission Impossible"
"As always, should you or any of your IM Force be caught or killed,
the Secretary will disavow any knowledge of your actions"

54

"Happenstance"

The Murder of

Eugene "Gino" Carrafa

In August of 1976, what started out as a missing person ended up as a multi-jurisdictional murder investigation culminating in a 142-page House Select Committee on Assassinations (HSCA) report. The report was derived from Maryland's Montgomery County Police Department's running resume on information accumulated during an investigation of the murder of Eugene "Gino" Michael Carrafa.

Eugene Carrafa, a resident of Montgomery County was the president of Gino's Classic Cars Inc., located in Harford County, Maryland. He was reported missing on August 1st by his wife, Carol. She told county police that her husband left for New York on July 28th to visit his partner, Jay Knohl, who resided in the Seagate section of Brooklyn, New York. According to Mrs. Carrafa her husband was going to California to check on the possibility of buying an antique car, and that Knohl was to give Carrafa money to seal the purchase.

On August 4th the New York City Police Department recovered Eugene Carrafa's body washed up on the shore of Great Kills Harbor in Staten Island. The body of the former Marine was found strangled and with loops of chains tied around his waist. The Montgomery County authorities were notified and entered the investigation. The county's Organized Crime Unit became interested in the Carrafa murder after the August 7th discovery of the body of Johnny Roselli floating in a drum off Biscayne Bay, Florida near Miami. The Organized Crime Unit wanted to investigate a possible connection between the two gangland style murders. The cause of death in both cases was asphyxiation, with both bodies weighted down and dumped in a body of water. Roselli was the Chicago Outfit's representative in Los Angeles and Las Vegas. He was intimately involved in the CIA's and the Mob's assassination attempts on Cuban Dictator Fidel Castro. Roselli had been summoned numerous times to testify before the HSCA concerning his knowledge of the assassination of President Kennedy.

Preliminary investigation in Carrafa's death by the Montgomery County authorities centered around an underground network involving valuable stolen antique cars worth hundreds of thousands of dollars. Carrafa's obscure antique car "sales and service" operation was almost never open for business. The investigation also found that Carrafa was one of several top-echelon racketeers in the Washington, D.C. area working with Joe Nesline and Charlie Tourine. Nesline and Tourine were both questioned regarding Carrafa's and Roselli's murders.

244

During the course of the investigation, it was determined that on July 28, 1976, Eugene Carrafa went to Jay G. Knohl's home in Brooklyn to collect a $10,000 debt. On August 4th, Carrafa's body was recovered from a harbor in Staten Island which was in a straight line from Jay Knohl's residence. According to tide tables the surfacing of the body was compatible to the disposition of the body from Knohl's waterfront property. When New York City detectives went to question Knohl about the recovered body, other detectives were already there to arrest Knohl on sex offense charges. Jay G. Knohl had an extensive arrest record dating back to 1956 and was a registered sex offender. Just like Johnny Roselli the murder of Eugene "Gino" Carrafa was never definitively solved.

The following are entries in the running resume of Carrafa's homicide investigation and was a part of the HSCA's report looking into the connection between the Carrafa and Roselli murders;

>On August 13, 1976, The NYPD received information from Dick Carlson, an investigative reporter at KFMB-TV in San Diego, California. The reporter stated he was informed by an anonymous source that "Carrafa met with John Roselli on the East Coast this year." The two murder victims also met in Chicago. The source could elaborate no further.

>On August 18, 1976, a reporter for Channel 5, New York City News apprised the NYPD that Carrafa was a "Hit Man" in Florida.

>On November 15, 1976, The NYPD Organized Crime unit advised that Jay G. Knohl ran a policy operation which was controlled by the Columbo Family.

>On February 27, 1977, Meyer Lansky, Charles "The Blade" Tourine, Joe Nesline and other Mob connected figures were subpoenaed to answer questions in Miami relative to the Roselli murder.

55

"Another Body Another Body of Water"

The Death of

"Handsome Johnny" Roselli

Fillippo Sacco

John "Handsome Johnny" Roselli

(photo CRIMEZINE)

On January 21, 1975, Senator John Pastore (D) Rhode Island, introduced a resolution to establish a select committee to investigate federal intelligence operations and determine "the extent, if any, to which illegal, improper, or unethical activities were engaged in by any agency of the Federal Government." The Senate approved the resolution on January 27, 1975. The committee was chaired by Senator Frank Church (D) Idaho. The "Church Committee" revealed the existence to the public of:

> "Family Jewels" a set of reports detailing illegal, inappropriate and otherwise sensitive activities conducted by the CIA from 1959 to 1973.

> "Operation Mongoose" CIA covert operations in Cuba, officially authorized by President Kennedy on November 30, 1961.

> "Operation MKULTRA" CIA mind control ops.

> "COINTELPRO" surveillance and infiltration of American political and civil-rights organizations.

> "OPERATION MOCKINGBIRD" propaganda campaign with US and foreign journalists operating as CIA assets.

Events Subsequent to the Church Committee Hearings;

> June 19, 1975, Sam "Momo" Giancana was killed in the basement of his Oak Park, Illinois home. He was shot with 7 bullets down his throat, a Mob message to informants. Giancana had been scheduled to testify, before the Church Committee. (According to a House Select Committee on Assassinations (HSCA) report dated August 13, 1976, former Washington D.C. Police Inspector Joseph Shimon met with Giancana and Roselli in a hotel room on New York Avenue, N.E. Washington, D.C. shortly before he was murdered in the basement of his Chicago home). The HSCA report also included an entry dated August 24, 1976. A confidential source (CI) advised Montgomery County Police, Sam Giancana stays at Joe Shimon's farm in Kitzmiller, Maryland when he comes to D.C.

> June 24, 1975, Johnny Roselli was summoned before the Church Committee to testify about his knowledge and participation in the plot to assassinate Fidel Castro, "Operation Mongoose." He testified before the committee but never sought permission to answer the summons from the Mafia Commission. Roselli was also summoned to appear before the House Select Committee on Assassinations about his knowledge of the assassination of President John F. Kennedy.

> July 30, 1975, Teamster Boss Jimmy Hoffa disappears.

> September 1975, Johnny Roselli was called back to testify again before the Senate Intelligence Committee.

> January 1976, Roselli testifies for the 3rd time before the Senate Intelligence Committee on the JFK murder.

> April 23, 1976, Roselli was summoned for a 4th time to testify before the HSCA. After his latest testimony, Roselli had become an embarrassment to the Mob and a "Hit" was authorized.

>July 27, 1976, Roselli was again summoned before the Assassination Committee. "Handsome Johnny Roselli" never appeared before the committee. Senator Howard Baker (R) Tennessee ordered the FBI to investigate Roselli's disappearance. Toll records revealed Roselli called Fred B. Black at his Watergate apartment in D.C., the day before he disappeared. Black was a super Washington, D.C. lobbyist with connections to President Lyndon Johnson, Bobby Baker (Johnson's bagman), Sam Giancana, Charlie Tourine, Joe Nesline and other nefarious personalities. On August 24, 1976, a confidential source (CI) advised

Montgomery County Police, Roselli stays at Fred Black's Watergate apartment when he comes to D.C.

> August 7, 1976, Roselli's body was found in Florida chopped up and stuffed in a 55-gallon barrel floating in Biscayne Bay, South Florida. The "Hit" on Roselli had been sanctioned by Anthony "Big Tuna" Accardo of the Chicago Outfit, the Mafia faction that Johnny Roselli answered to. (According to the same HSCA report dated August 13, 1976, Roselli's long distance toll records revealed he called former D.C. Police official Joe Shimon at his Garrett County, Maryland home telephone number.

> On March 29, 1977, Charles "Chuckie" Nicoletti, Chicago Outfit assassin and righthand man to Sam Giancana and a suspect in his murder, was found dead sitting in his car in Northlake, Illinois with three gunshot wounds to the back of the head. He was due to testify that same day before the House Select Committee on Assassinations. Another suspect in Giancana's death was Charles James Tourine Jr. aka Chuckie Delmonico the son of Charlie Tourine. Delmonico also had access to Sam Giancana's home. Tourine Jr. died of natural causes while serving a long sentence in an Atlanta penitentiary in 2008.

"Once is happenstance
Twice is Coincidence
Three Times is Enemy Action"
Ian Fleming

56

"Self-Inflicted"

The Death of

Gabriel D. Bobrow

In December 1978, Gabriel "Gabby" D. Bobrow, a District of Columbia businessman whom U.S. officials had linked to narcotics and organized crime figures, was found dead in his apartment. A neighbor alerted the police after hearing a gun-shot. Police found Bobrow shot through the head in his ninth-floor apartment at 2130 P Street N.W. A revolver was found near the body. Police considered the death of the 45-year-old Bobrow to be self-inflicted.

"Gabby" Bobrow's criminal record revealed considerable involvement with the law, including several past convictions for drug offenses and being a fugitive from justice for warrants issued in New York. In 1965, Justice Department prosecutors in Washington, D.C. were investigating Joe Nesline as the leader of organized criminal activities in the Washington metropolitan area. They granted Bobrow immunity and he testified before a special grand jury investigating interstate gambling. Bobrow acknowledged a business relationship with Nesline, but denied any organized crime ties to him. Bobrow once managed the Washington Wig Co., an enterprise that had been owned by Nesline.

Bobrow was sentenced in 1972 to six years in prison for possession of cocaine and marijuana with intent to distribute. At the time, federal drug enforcement officials described him as a wholesaler of narcotics with close ties to two of the area's top 10 heroin wholesalers. When arrested in Alexandria, Virginia, he was driving an expensive car and had in his possession significant amounts of cocaine, heroin and marijuana with an estimated street value in excess of $100,000 and more than $5,000 in cash. Subsequent searches uncovered additional drugs and paraphernalia commonly employed in testing the purity of narcotics and in preparing them for sale.

Bobrow was a Polish national and was classified as an undesirable alien, but was never deported. At the time it was official U.S. government policy not to deport to communist-controlled countries.

57

"Casino Consultant"

Prominent Investors

Nathan Landow

(photo The Washington Post)

On January 14 1978, federal and local police raided Joe Nesline's apartment in Bethesda, Maryland as part of a federal investigation of gambling. Law enforcement agencies had been planning the raid for more than a year. It was one of many conducted simultaneously in cities throughout the country including Las Vegas. FBI agents seized a file containing correspondence spelling out a proposed $85 million deal involving Nathan Landow and Smith Bagley. The two prominent Washington investors were involved in a proposal to build a hotel and gambling casino in Atlantic City. At the time, Nesline lived in the luxurious Promenade high-rise apartment building owned by Nathan Landow at 5225 Pooks Hill Road in Bethesda, Maryland. When pressed to explain how the file and

253

its contents came to be found in his possession, Nesline admitted to officers that he had been acting as a "consultant" in the casino venture.

Nathan Landow was a self-made entrepreneur and multi-millionaire builder. He was a heavy contributor to the Democratic Party and an active fund-raiser for President Carter. Before news of the raids were publicized, he was under consideration for appointment as U.S. ambassador to the Netherlands. In a Washington Post article, Nathan Landow acknowledged knowing Nesline but he did not know him to be an important illegal gambling figure. Landow and his lawyer Saul Schwartzbach consulted with Nesline to gain expertise in order for Landow and Bagley to negotiate knowledgeably in what was to be a joint venture with Resorts International Inc. Schwartzbach said he went to Nesline to find out what it would take to set up a casino and what profits could be made. Bagley was also quoted in the article in reference to Nesline, "I have never met this man I never heard of this man." Landow brought Bagley into the prospective deal because U.S. financial institutions traditionally shied away from lending to Casino operations. It was anticipated that Bagley would be able to find financing through Middle Eastern contacts that he had made socially on Washington's embassy circuit.

The New Jersey State Police interviewed Nathan Landow, to learn what Joe Nesline's role was in the Atlantic City Casino deal. Landow stated, "Look, if I'd known Prince Rainier, I would have gone to him because his casino and his knowledge of the operation was probably a lot more than Joe Nesline's. If I knew the Tisch brothers from the Lewis Hotel chain, they have a very successful hotel-casino in Monte Carlo. I would have gone to MGM. I would have gone to the Sheraton people. I would have gone to Mr. Rockefeller, who operates a casino in Dorado Beach (Puerto Rico). But I didn't know any of them."

Neither Schwartzbach nor Landow could explain how the copy of the letter to the Atlantic City Housing Authority came to be in Nesline's possession. Schwartzbach said he may have given the copy to Nesline during the meeting. Nesline probably took notes while they were talking. Schwartzbach said, explaining that this could account for the handwritten memoranda found by the police.

The Altlantic City hotel-casino project was not the only gambling venture in which Nesline had been involved with Landow. Also found in the raid of Nesline's apartment was an architectural rendering for another proposed hotel-casino deal on the Caribbean Island of Sint Maarten's in which Nesline was acting as a middleman. Sint Maarten is a constituent country of the Kingdom of the Netherlands. Also involved in the Sint Maarten's venture with Nesline and Landow was Edward Cellini, the brother of Dino Cellini, Nesline's old friend from Steubenville Ohio and "Jimmy's Place." Edward Cellini was already operating one hotel casino, The Concord, on Sint Maarten when he and Landow were brought together by Nesline in 1976. Dino Cellini and other family members were listed in a Rolodex that was confiscated by police in the gambling raid at Nesline's apartment.

For assistance in funding for the proposed casino on Sint Maarten, Landow turned to an old friend Lester Matz. Matz was a Maryland construction engineer who admitted paying cash kickbacks to public officials including Spiro T. Agnew in order to obtain contracts for his firm. Matz was a key figure in the investigation that led to the resignation of Agnew, as Vice President. Matz was given immunity from prosecution for his information against Agnew.

In November 1978, Nathan Landow gave a dinner party for actress Shirley Maclaine that attracted more than 200 people to Landow's Bethesda home. Among the guests were some of President Carter's family as well as members of his administration and other democratic politicians. The party at Landow's home was observed by Montgomery County, Maryland police officers of the organized crime section. They had Landow under surveillance for nearly a year. They had learned from Florida police that Landow had a financial interest in a defunct corporation whose silent partners allegedly included an identified member of the "Carlo Gambino Mafia family." The business involvement of Landow's that originally attracted the attention of Montgomery County's organized crime unit was an investment in Quaker Masonry Inc., a firm that had offices in Silver Spring, Maryland and Hollywood, Florida. Landow was listed in 1972 as a vice president and director of Quaker Masonry. Florida authorities reported that Anthony Plate, known to them to be an associate of the Gambinos was believed to have a 25 percent interest in Quaker. Landow had invested between $120.000 and $160.000 in Quaker. Landow said he had seen Plate at Quaker when he went down on an inspection trip.

In the early 1970s, agents from the IRS and FBI came to Landow to ask questions and alert him that they were watching Nesline. The inquiries began when Nesline first moved into the Colonnade, another luxury high-rise that Landow built on New Mexico Avenue, N.W. The inquiries continued after he sold the Colonnade and Nesline and other tenants moved out to the Promenade. Internal Revenue agents examined Landow's rental records pertaining to Nesline. His two-bedroom apartment was in the name of a girlfriend and paid less than other tenants in similar apartments and always in cash.

Joe Nesline had offered many favors to Landow and his family through the years. He arranged for Landow's elderly parents to take a free trip to Yugoslavia, where Nesline ran a casino. Since Nesline had a financial interest in a casino in Las Vegas, Landow would often ask Nesline to make reservations which enabled him to stay free. One summer, when Landow took his wife and three children to Europe, they discovered the hotel they had booked was not to Mrs. Landow's taste and she refused to unpack, insisting that her husband "Call Joe". Nesline, who was staying a few blocks away at Loews Monte Carlo, one of Europe's very first hotels and resorts with an onsite casino, arranged for the Landows to get better accommodations there.

Smith Bagley

(photo New York Times)

Smith Bagley was heir to the R.J. Reynolds tobacco fortune. He was a major contributor to national Democratic candidates. His Musgrove Plantation on St. Simon's Island off the coast of Georgia had served as Jimmy Carter's presidential vacation retreat. Bagley was also in line for several diplomatic posts, including U.S. chief of protocol and U.S. ambassador to Great Britain. Bagley accused The Washington Post of bias and unethical conduct in its coverage of the Atlantic City hotel casino proposal. "Ever since Maxine Cheshire (author of the Post article) asked me for a $25,000 personal loan and I turned her down, I have felt my family and I have been under a magnifying glass with Washington Post eyes looking through it." Cheshire and Post managing editors Ben Bradlee and Harry M. Rosenfeld all disputed Bagley's allegations.

58

"Recovered Rolodex"

Honorable Mentions

During the January 14, 1978 federal raid on Joe Nesline's apartment in Bethesda, Maryland, the Feds seized documents and correspondence relating to gambling operations involving Nesline and other targeted individuals. Among the items seized was Joe Nesline's telephone rolodex, which contained a list of national and international names and contact information on many of his associates, codefendants, lawyers and business partners mentioned in previous chapters.

The following is a cast of questionable characters and entities contained in Nesline's rolodex not previously mentioned;

Ernest Anastas;

Ernest Anastas was a Detroit, Michigan racketeer associated with Joe Nesline in arranging gambling junkets to legal casinos. In June 1977, William Lucas, a Democrat Wayne County, Michigan Sheriff was one of several candidates considered by President Jimmy Carter to head the Federal Bureau of Investigation. Sheriff Lucas was dropped as a viable contender after Bureau agents investigated his background. On June 24, the investigators leaked to the New York Post Lucas' admission of accepting free gambling junkets to Las Vegas and of having as his traveling companion Ernest Anastas. The racketeer had been indicted in 1970 on Federal gambling conspiracy charges. The case ended in a mistrial and Mr. Anastas was never retried.

In 1986, William Lucas, now the Wayne County Executive, switched to the Republican Party and announced his candidacy for Governor of Michigan. Wayne County includes the city of Detroit. Lucas found himself having to deal with conflict-of-interest charges in his county office and with recycled news reports of his acceptance of free trips to Las Vegas from Anastas in 1977. William Lucas lost the election to incumbent Democrat Governor James J. Blanchard. William Lucas would have been the first African American Governor of Michigan.

Isaac Irving Davidson;

Isaac Irving Davidson came to Washington, D.C. from Pittsburgh in 1941 to work for the War Production Board. In 1944, he began working in public relations and later he became a licensed arms dealer arranging arms deals for Anastasio Somoza of Nicaragua, Fulgencio Batista of Cuba and various other despots around the world. He was also a mobster's dream. Davidson was a close associate of New Orleans Mafia Boss Carlos Marcello, Miami Boss Santos Trafficante, New York Boss Frank Costello and D.C. Mob associate Joe Nesline among others. He played an important role in the legal attempt to prevent Jimmy Hoffa from being sent to prison. Davidson was the epitome of the Washington lobbyist; a schemer and promoter with a vast international network of powerful acquaintances.

He liked to refer to himself as "a door opener and arranger" and as "grease for the machinery." Davidson was a specialist in "putting people together." He was a "Bag Man" for the Mafia, the Teamsters Union, the FBI, the CIA and the NSC (National Security Council). In Washington, Davidson shared an office with investigative journalists, Jack Anderson and Drew Pearson and was a constant source of information for Anderson's syndicated columns.

Deak & Company Washington Inc.;

The firm Deak & Company was founded in 1939 by Nicolas Louis Deák. In the 1930s he immigrated to New York City from Transylvania (now Romania). Deak served in World War II in the Office of Strategic Services, where he operated behind enemy lines under the command of William (Wild Bill) Donovan, and performed intelligence work throughout Southeast Asia and southern Europe. Nick Deak returned to New York in 1946 with the financial backing of the CIA. He soon became known as the "James Bond of Money." For more than three decades the company had functioned as an unofficial arm of the intelligence agency and was a key asset in the execution of U.S. Cold War foreign policy. The firm grew to become possibly the largest currency and precious metals firm in the world.

His worldwide financial group was shaken in the late '70s and early '80s by multiple scandals involving money laundering and criminal connections. In 1984, Deak & Company faced allegations from the President's Commission on Organized Crime that the firm laundered money for Latin American drug traffickers, facilitated bribes for the Lockheed corporation and smuggled currency from the Philippines.

The report of the President's Commission offers some glimpses into a peculiar world of high finance.

> From 1969 to 1975, Deak & Company was the conduit used by the Lockheed Corporation to transfer money intended by Lockheed to bribe Japanese officials. The bribery scandal resulted in the criminal conviction of a former Japanese Prime Minister. Deak & Company moved $8.3 million to Japan via Hong Kong.

> In 1978 Deak & Company and one of its vice presidents were convicted on criminal charges of willfully failing to file reports on about $11 million deposited by two Philippine businessmen.

> The most serious charges involve the "laundering" of tens of millions of dollars amassed by cocaine traffickers. Investigators for the commission identified the "Grandma Mafia," a well-known cocaine ring that involved middle-aged or elderly women, as being used to deposit $7.6 million. The money was later transferred to Miami, Panama and Colombia. The ringleaders of the "Grandma Mafia" were arrested and prosecuted in Los Angeles.

> Another case involved $97 million, largely cocaine profits, deposited in Deak & Company subsidiaries' accounts between 1980 and 1982. Millions of dollars were often brought to the company's lower Manhattan office, in cash packed in cardboard boxes.

On November 18, 1985, a mentally unstable and homeless woman, entered Nicolas Deak's office and shot and killed both Deak and his receptionist. When arrested the woman claimed that she was a part owner of Deak & Company and said that she had suffered some injustice from the company. She was initially institutionalized and later sent to a Correctional Facility. Subsequent to the murder of Nicolas Deak, theories have been suggested that he was targeted for assassination, because of his work for the intelligence community and the company's involvement with money laundering.

Lawrence V. Meyers;

Lawrence Meyers was associated with Joe Nesline when they were involved in arranging gambling junkets to casinos in the Caribbean. He was originally from New York City and settled in Chicago as a teenager. Meyers' legitimate employment was as a sales manager for various sporting goods manufacturing companies. He had business interests in various California cities as well as Memphis, Tennessee, Minneapolis, Minnesota, Las Vegas, Nevada, and Dallas, Texas. While in Dallas, Meyers befriended Jack Ruby while frequenting Ruby's Carousel Club which featured striptease artists. Jack Ruby (Jacob Leon Rubenstein) is the killer of Lee Harvey Oswald, the assassin of President John F. Kennedy.

The Warren Commission considered Lawrence Meyers to be a personal friend of Jack Ruby. The Warren Commission was officially known as The President's Commission on the Assassination of President Kennedy and the Death of Lee

Harvey Oswald. It was set up pursuant to an Executive Order issued by President Lynden B. Johnson. In August 1964, Lawrence V. Meyers was summoned by the commission to give a deposition in order to examine the extent of his friendship with Ruby. The deposition was taken in Washington, D.C. at an office building on Capitol Hill adjacent to the Supreme Court. The commission wanted to concentrate on conversations Ruby and Meyers had, both shortly before the assassination and shortly afterwards, including the shooting of Oswald by Ruby.

Within the 20-page statement given during Lawrence Meyers' deposition, he gave the impression of being fully cooperative, but revealed very little of any substance. Topics of discussion between Ruby and Meyers included Ruby's business conflicts with several other striptease club owners in Dallas and getting no satisfaction from the American Guild of Variety Artists (AGVA). The only relevant statement Meyers made to the commission was his discussion with Ruby about President Kennedy. Jack Ruby worshipped Kennedy and his family. According to Meyers, after President Kennedy was assassinated Ruby repeated a number of times, "those poor people, those poor people, I have got to do something" or, "I should do something about this." Lee Harvey Oswald's name was never mentioned by Ruby.

Nicholas Katsouros and Roger W. "Roddy" Simkins Jr.;
NicholasKatsouros and Roger "Roddy" Simkins were both targeted by the Feds and the D.C. Metropolitan Police Department. Between the late 1970s and the early 1980s, these law enforcement agencies conducted a series of raids on

homes and offices associated with Katsouros and Simkins Jr., as well as locations in Ocean City, Maryland and Las Vegas Nevada. They were arrested and charged with conspiracy, running major million-dollar illegal sports bookmaking operations, tax-related offences, marijuana and weapons offences.

One of the first raids by D.C. police on "Roddy" Simkins was executed on the eve of the 1978 Super Bowl football game. "Roddy", along with a Las Vegas based codefendant were charged with conspiracy and gambling. They were eventually acquitted. The defense lawyer contended the case against Roddy Simkins stemmed from a long-running effort by the Internal Revenue Service to locate and tax large sums of illegal gambling profits that the agency believes Roddy's father hid before his death in 1973. Roddy's father was Roger "Whitetop" Simkins one of D.C.'s most prominent gambling figures of the 1940s and 1950s. "Whitetop" would eventually serve three years in prison for bribing police officers to look the other way.

Salvatore Santoro;

Salvatore T. "Tom Mix" Santoro, Sr. served as underboss in the Lucchese crime family during the 1980s before being convicted in New York's Mafia Commission Trial along with "Fat Tony" Salerno and others. He acquired the nickname "Tom Mix" because in his younger years he closely resembled the western film actor by that name. In Nesline's rolodex, Santoro was listed under his nickname, "Tom Mix."

As a Capo, Santoro operated out of East Harlem and the Bronx, controlling large heroin drug trafficking operations during the 1950s. In 1958 he was arrested and tried for narcotics charges. He was alleged to be a partner and associate of "The Godfather of Harlem," Ellsworth "Bumpy" Johnson.

Odessa Madre;

Odessa was dubbed "The Lady Al Capone of Washington, D.C." and the "Queen of the Washington Underworld." Odessa Madre, a Black woman, operated in male-dominated circles for nearly 50 years. She was highly intelligent and street-smart as well as book-smart. In 1925, she began her life of crime at 17 because she knew that "crime did pay." She thrived in the criminal environment for decades, which is largely due to the fact she grew up in the low-income multi-ethnic, mostly Irish and Black, neighborhood of D.C.'s Cowtown (a name given because of the slaughterhouses and cows roamed the streets and small alleyways). The two groups never fought each other, but they did fight together against other poor immigrant kids from neighboring areas. These early relationships helped her crime syndicate grow into an empire because many of her Irish childhood friends went on to become officials who filled the ranks of the Metropolitan Police Department.

Madre knew all the big-name gangsters in the city, and her connections in law enforcement looked the other way. She set aside "ice," or protection payments for the cops. During her heyday in the 1930s and '40s, she was earning $100,000 a year with her various enterprises. She controlled gambling, narcotics, bootleg whiskey and managed up to six brothels at one time. Her most prominent venture was amusing notable celebrities at her infamous nightclub, Club Madre, located on D.C.'s old "Red Light District, the 14th Street Strip in N.W. The club once entertained Count Basie, Nat King Cole and Heavyweight Champion Joe Louis among other notables.

It all came to an end when her free passes from the police department were exposed in 1952, when the Kefauver Committee cracked down on the corruption and Madre's payments of "Ice" protection money was revealed. Odessa Madre, one of the richest, most flamboyant, big-hearted hustlers who ever worked the shadier side of the Nation's Capitol, died penniless at age 83.

59

"Contempt of Court"

The Judge Alcee Hastings Case

U.S. District Court Judge for the State of Florida

Alcee Lamar Hastings

(photo Nova Law Review)

U.S. Congressman Alcee Hastings of Florida was a U.S. District Judge for the Southern District of Florida from 1979 to 1989. In 1981, Joe Nesline was jailed in Miami for contempt of court for refusing to answer questions before a grand jury that was investigating bribery allegations involving Judge Hastings. The backstory of the Hastings` bribery investigation may have been a larger alleged payoff scheme that involved Florida Mob boss Santo Trafficante Jr.

Alcee Hastings was a prominent South Florida attorney who was serving as a Florida Circuit Court Judge when he was appointed to the federal bench in 1979 by President Jimmy Carter. He was the first African American to be appointed a federal judge in the state of Florida. His problems began in 1981 after the case of two brothers, Frank and Thomas Romano, who were accused of stealing over $1 million from the New Jersey Teamsters pension fund.

The Romano brothers, natives of Mistretta, Sicily, were builders in Hallandale, Florida. They were indicted in 1980 for mail and wire fraud, theft, embezzlement and racketeering after an FBI sting operation. The brothers had been tried and convicted in Hastings' courtroom for pocketing money loaned from the New Jersey Teamsters Union. The money was supposed to be used for construction of the Executive House condominium in Lauderhill, Florida.

In June 1981, Mob Boss Santo Trafficante Jr., Anthony "Big Tuna" Accardo and 13 others pleaded innocent to federal racketeering indictments. All of the men were charged with conspiracy under the RICO act after a three-year investigation into the insurance plans of the Laborers' International Union of North America (LIUNA). The defendants, including officers of LIUNA, allegedly split hundreds of thousands of dollars received from kickbacks from insurance companies, a scheme that was ongoing since 1973. The U.S. Magistrate taking the pleas set a trial date in July 1981, before U.S. District Court Judge Alcee Hastings.

In July 1981, while the Romanos were awaiting sentencing, William C. Dredge, the owner of a Miami antique store, who was also a burglar, fence and drug dealer, turned up in the office of the U.S. attorney in Miami. He was under indictment in Baltimore, Maryland for distributing Quaaludes. He said he wanted to avoid jail, and had good information to trade. He knew of a Washington, D.C. attorney who claimed to be able to fix cases in the courtroom of Alcee Hastings. Dredge said that the attorney, William Borders, a close friend of Hastings, was the go-between, acting to collect the bribe money and pass it on to Hastings. In addition, Dredge said that Borders was interested in soliciting a bribe for Hastings from the Romano brothers, and had asked Dredge to see if the brothers were willing to pay Hastings in exchange for no jail time and having their forfeited ill-gotten gains returned.

Dredge met Borders through Joseph Nesline in Washington D.C. In July, 1981, Dredge was staying at Nesline's home while pending trial in his Baltimore drug case. Santo Trafficante Jr. was also a guest of Nesline's. While at Nesline's apartment William Dredge overheard Trafficante calling William Borders. Dredge went to dinner with Nesline, Trafficante and Nesline's wife at Le Lion D'Or, at the time a landmark French restaurant on Connecticut Avenue. Dredge and Nesline's wife sat at an adjoining table next to Nesline and Trafficante. Dredge learned that Trafficante was in town to see William Borders about a bribe to fix his criminal case pending before Judge Hastings. Dredge alleged that Trafficante had agreed to pay $600,000 to Hastings through Borders to fix his racketeering charge. Dredge went on to say that Borders had contacted him about arranging for Tom and Frank Romano to pay a $150,000 bribe to have Hastings reduce their jail sentences to probation.

William A. Borders Jr., was president of the predominantly Black National Bar Association. Borders was a fund raiser for President Jimmy Carter in 1976 and 1980, and Carter appointed Borders to a panel that selected judges for federal Districts. In 1979, when the Carter administration created a search committee for several new federal judgeships, Borders was consulted on promising minority appointees, and recommended the nomination of Hastings, a friend of almost 20 years.

At the request of the Miami U.S. Attorney's office the FBI initiated an investigation. On July 21, 1981 they set up a surveillance at the Miami Airport. Borders arrived in Miami and was followed by agents as he took a cab to Dredge's house. Dredge then drove Borders to a shopping center where Borders took a cab to the Fontainebleau Hotel. Borders was observed meeting with Santo Trafficante for five to ten minutes. Trafficante then drove Borders back to the airport. Agents observed Trafficante shake Borders' hand and heard him say "did a good job." Trafficante left Borders at the airport. Borders caught a flight back to Washington. The Feds then decided on an undercover operation involving the Romano brothers. Dredge told the FBI, Borders had asked him to approach Frank and Thomas Romano and solicit a bribe, offering low sentences and the return of nearly $1 million in property that Hastings had ordered them to forfeit. The Romanos declined to cooperate, Dredge believed the brothers may have made their own deal with Judge Hastings. The FBI decided to move forward with the Sting operation by introducing an undercover agent to impersonate Frank Romano. The bureau brought out of retirement former FBI organized crime agent, H. Paul Rico who was roughly the right age and bearing. Dredge performed the introduction, and Borders took the bait.

The retired undercover FBI agent (UC), posing as Frank Romano, approached Borders to say that yes, the Romanos were interested in paying off Hastings in return for light treatment. Borders said it could be done. When Borders said that, the UC indicated he wanted to go ahead with the deal, but had some questions: How would the UC know if Borders really spoke for Hastings? Can Borders arrange some sort of sign to show that Hastings was on board? Borders said, he could have Hastings show up somewhere at the time and place of the UC's choosing. Borders and the UC agreed that Hastings could give the signal by coming to the dining room of the Fontainebleau Hotel at 8:00 P.M. on September 16, 1981. If Hastings did show up at that appointed place and time, then everyone would know he was part of the deal.

When the time came, FBI agents had the hotel under surveillance. And sure enough, Hastings showed up for dinner at eight. The FBI did extensive investigation to determine whether Hastings might have gone to the Fontainebleau by chance, or whether Borders, who on that night was in Las Vegas watching a prizefight, might have tricked Hastings into it. They found nothing to support that theory. As far as the Feds were concerned the signal was sent; Hastings was on board.

A deal was struck. In a meeting at the Miami airport, the UC gave Borders $25,000 as a down payment. In return, Hastings was to throw out the forfeiture judgment against the Romanos. After that, the rest of the money, $125,000, would be paid. Hastings did indeed throw out the judgment, and showed particular interest in making sure it was done quickly. "I want the order today," he told his law clerk, according to testimony in the case. "Sorry for the rush, but the order has to go out today." A short time later, a pickup date for the full payoff was set.

On October 9, 1981, the day William Borders was to be honored in Washington for the end of his tenure as head of the National Bar Association, he got a call to meet (UC) "Frank" at the Twin Bridges Marriott in Arlington, Virginia. Borders showed up and met with the FBI agent he thought was Frank Romano. The agent had brought the $125,000. When the money changed hands, Borders was immediately arrested.

Hastings was also in Washington that day to attend the dinner honoring his friend. Borders had made Hastings' hotel reservation at the L'Enfant Plaza, and spent the morning with the judge. When Hastings heard that Borders had been nabbed, and that the FBI wanted to talk to him, Hastings quickly changed his plans. A later law review article on the case described Hastings's actions this way: "Hastings was at the L'Enfant Plaza Hotel in Washington, D.C. when he heard the news of

Borders' arrest. His reaction was to leave Washington immediately and return to Florida, thereby avoiding the FBI. He quickly packed a bag and left the hotel without checking out, leaving behind a suit he had sent to the hotel's valet service. The suit was retrieved by the FBI several days later. Instead of going to National Airport in Washington, a short drive from his hotel, Hastings took a long, expensive cab ride to Baltimore-Washington International (BWI) airport. Once there, he called his mother in Florida from a pay phone. Hastings then placed a collect call from a second pay phone at the airport to the home of his girlfriend, Patricia Williams. The call lasted a minute or less. Hastings told Williams to call him back at a third pay phone, which she did. He then told her to go to a pay phone and call him again at the same number. About fifteen minutes later, she called Hastings from a pay phone located in a shopping mall near her home. This call lasted a minute or less. Hastings then called her at the mall pay phone from a fourth pay phone at the BWI Airport. This call lasted about four minutes. After that, Hastings caught a plane south. The FBI found him late that night at his girlfriend's house."

In December 1981, Hastings was indicted, charged with conspiring with Borders to solicit a bribe from the Romanos. Borders was also indicted. At trial, Hastings pleaded not guilty and claimed Borders was lying about the whole thing. He also claimed the prosecution was racially motivated. Borders was swiftly convicted on March 29, 1982, and sentenced to five years in jail and a $35,000 fine. Borders' lawyers argued that media coverage has suggested their client "has a nefarious relationship" with reputed mobster Santo Trafficante Jr. and Washington, D.C.,

274

gambler Joseph Nesline. Hastings, after a separate three-week trial, was acquitted. The jury of six men and six women, after deliberating 17 1/2 hours, concluded that the government had not established Hastings' guilt beyond a reasonable doubt.

When the appeals court reversed the Romanos' convictions, it said it was doing so because of an error made by Hastings, and not because there was not enough evidence against them. The government seized the $1.2 million in May 1981. Hastings returned $845,000 to the Romanos on October 6, 1981.

The abrupt arrest forced the Feds to go to court with a strictly circumstantial case. Hastings responded with the defense which he always maintained: that William Borders was indeed conspiring to solicit bribes in Hastings' courtroom, but without the judge's knowledge. No dirty money was ever found and the FBI found no signs that Hastings' lifestyle was out of the ordinary, for a man earning, in 1981, $70,300 a year.

Nesline was called to testify before a federal grand jury in Miami, investigating bribery allegations involving Judge Hastings. Despite being given immunity, Nesline refused to testify. His attorney contended that he was taking medications that could possibly impair his memory.

U.S. District Judge Sidney Aronovitz ruled the medical reasons were not sufficient and found Nesline in contempt-of-court. On December 4, 1981, Nesline was

275

taken to the Federal Correctional Institute. The Judge ordered Nesline incarcerated for 18 months or until he agreed to testify.

The immunity granted Nesline was the first sought by federal prosecutors during the four and one-half month investigation of Hastings. During his appearance before the grand jury, Nesline invoked the Fifth Amendment. At that point, the judge allowed Nesline's attorney to study overnight the government's motion to find Nesline in civil contempt. Aronovitz advised the attorney "Tell your client to bring his toothbrush." Nesline was released after serving 8 months of his 18-month sentence.

Hastings was acquitted in his federal trial but was later impeached, convicted, and removed from office by the United States Senate. Borders also refused to co-operate with the impeachment proceedings against Judge Hastings. Hastings turned the notoriety of his federal trial to his advantage and was elected to Congress. As a Congressman, Hastings was a staunch supporter of President Clinton during his impeachment proceedings. President Clinton pardoned William Borders and he returned to Washington after 33 months in Allenwood Penitentiary. The only man who could conclusively clear or implicate Alcee Hastings, declined to testify. Hastings died of pancreatic cancer on April 6, 2021.

In 2003, retired FBI undercover agent H. Paul Rico was indicted for murder in Oklahoma and Florida for helping Boston Irish mobster "Whitey" Bulger and others plan the assassination of a wealthy Oklahoma businessman in 1981.

276

Rico died of congestive heart failure on January 16, 2004 in a Tulsa hospital where he was moved to from prison, still under indictment for the 1981 murder. He was 78.

In 2012, a book was published titled; "RICO- How Politicians, Prosecutors, and the Mob Destroyed one of the FBI's finest Special Agents." The book was written by two retired FBI Agents Joseph Wolfinger and Christopher Kerr and a journalist Jerry Seper. The authors concluded the case against Rico and the myth of his involvement in the 1981 murder was the concoction of two desperate Boston mobsters. More than that, they detail how the false charges that led to Rico's indictment was a perfect storm of corruption, ambition, raw politics and incompetence.

60

"Operation VIDGAM"

Myron Sugerman

Myron Sugarman

"The Last Jewish Gangster"

(photo Mob Museum)

In 1986, Joe Nesline was arrested at his Silver Spring, Maryland home along with three other codefendants. The arrests were subsequent to a joint FBI / Metropolitan Police investigation code named "Operation VIDGAM." They were charged with interstate transportation in aid of racketeering-gambling, interstate transportation of gambling devices, distribution of copies infringing the copyright of audio-visual works, and trafficking in goods using a counterfeit mark (a patent violation).

"Operation VIDGAM," was a spinoff of an earlier investigation in which an undercover agent was introduced to Nesline, who in turn introduced the agent to reputed gambling figures in the state of New Jersey. The Washington Post reported on the arrests in a January, 1987, article by Nancy Lewis. The reporter starts the article with the following paragraph: "Joseph F. Nesline, an admitted gambler for 65 of his 73 years and long considered the "Dean of D.C. Racketeers," pleaded guilty yesterday in federal court here to helping arrange the interstate shipment of a video poker game from New Jersey to the District."

The first indictment charged Joe Nesline and Walter F. "Buster" Riggin with distributing 11 "unlawfully manufactured and authorized copies" of video games, such as Donkey Kong and Ms. PacMan. The second indictment charged Joe Nesline, Myron Sugarman and Alan P. Fishkin, both from New Jersey, with distributing and transporting a variety of illegal video and gambling games from New Jersey to the District between July and December of 1985.

According to the indictment, Sugerman supplied the FBI undercover agent with the games and told the agent to place them in businesses in the Washington area and "funnel the money received from the illegal machines into legitimate businesses." The counterfeit video games looked identical to legitimate ones but were made with pirated parts, circumventing copyright and trademark laws and depriving the manufacturers of royalty payments. Nesline pleaded guilty to a single count of interstate transportation in aid of racketeering and in exchange the government promised not to ask for a prison sentence. He faced a maximum term of five years in prison and a $250,000 fine.

At the beginning of the trial, Nesline's lawyer sought to have Joe declared incompetent to stand trial because of memory problems. The federal Judge accepted Nesline's guilty plea after ruling that Nesline's memory problem is "not any more severe or any greater than anyone else's his age." According to a medical/psychiatric report filed with the court, doctors found; "Nesline exhibited some "antisocial" tendencies and showed a special disdain for "snitching." "In this regard, Mr. Nesline reports that he lives by a rule that he will give no information regarding his friends, associates or others because he doesn't talk about his relationships with others." Under the plea agreement, Nesline did not have to. Government prosecutors agreed not to call him as a witness in any future trial.

One of the New Jersey Gambling figures arrested with Joe Nesline was Myron Sugerman. Myron grew up in Maplewood, New Jersey and was the son of Barney "Sugie" Sugerman, a man who partnered in the gambling business with such notorious mob figures as Meyer Lansky and fellow Jerseyan Abner "Longie" Zwillman. Myron followed in his father's footsteps in the family business, selling and operating slot machines, jukeboxes and anything else that accepted coins and entertained people in venues all over the world.

In 2017, Myron Sugerman wrote a memoir, "The Chronicles of The Last Jewish Gangster: From Meyer to Myron." The book is an account of his nearly sixty-year career as an "international outlaw" in the field of slot machines and casinos. The memoir follows Sugerman's life from 1959 to the present day. He toured and lectured on his book and life to mostly Jewish organizations. In his lectures, Sugarman talked about doing business with some of the most dangerous characters known to the public, including members of the New York Genovese and Gambino Crime families, the Japanese Yakuza, the Columbian Cali Cartel and other ethnic criminal organizations.

In his chronicles, Myron Sugarman talks of his arrest in Washington, D.C. Before entering into the deal with Joe Nesline, Sugarman made enquiries about Joe Nesline's trustworthiness. He was assured by "Old-School" mobsters that Nesline could be trusted. Joe Nesline had a long-standing reputation with the old mobsters as a "Standup Guy." Sugarman bore no animosity towards Nesline after the arrests. At the time Joe was in his seventies and Myron figured Joe's mental faculties were not what they once were.

Joe Nesline's other co-defendant in "Operation VIDGAM" was Walter F. "Buster" Riggin. "Buster" Riggin was a long-time associate of Nesline. At the time of his video game counterfeiting arrest, he was the owner of B&B News located on Connecticut Avenue, N.W. Washington, D.C. "Buster" was a lifelong D.C. resident and just like Joe, nearly a lifelong criminal. His adult arrest record started with larcenies in the 1940s, burglaries in the 1960s, child pornography, racketeering and bribery in the 1970s and illegal gambling in the 1980s.

By the turn of the 21st century "Buster" became the proprietor of an "edgy" storefront business, K&B Newsstand located at 1004 F Street N.W. In October

2008, inspectors from D.C.'s Department of Consumer and Regulatory Affairs paid a visit to the business along with the Metropolitan Police. Based on their inspection "Buster" was arrested for selling stun guns which at the time were banned under D.C. law and classified as destructive devices. The inspectors also determined that the entire store was unlicensed to do business.

Epilogue

"I thought we'd be dead
by now"

In the plot synopsis for the 2000 black comedy crime film "The Crew" starring Richard Dreyfus and Burt Reynolds a quote reads: "Back in the days when mobsters were larger than life, none lived bigger than Bobby, "Bats", "The Brick" and "Mouth." But now well into retirement, the old crew find themselves suddenly facing eviction from their run-down Miami Beach hotel - The Raj Mahal. That's when they decided there's only one thing left to do - turn back the clock and pull one last "hit" in order to save their home."

The opening scene of the movie shows the aging Mob Crew members sitting outside their beach front hotel watching and commenting on a younger generation rollerblading, cruising and frolicking on the beach:

Joey "Bats" Pistella: (Burt Reynolds)
"I thought you said the good times were gonna last forever".
Bobby Bartellemeo: (Richard Dreyfus)
"I thought we'd be dead by now".

283

Charlie Tourine

In the 1950s, Charlie Tourine was living a lush life style with a swanky pad on Manhattan's Central Park south. He was known as a real Casanova, married six times and always with a new girl on his arm while making the rounds of all the hot spots. He worked with other connected casino operators in places like Puerto Rico and Antigua. Tourine traveled extensively with frequent trips to Europe, the Middle East and regularly returned back to New York City and Washington D.C.

By the 1970s, Tourine was semi-retired and living in Miami, Florida. When the decomposed remains of "Handsome" Johnny Roselli were fished out of Biscayne Bay in 1976, police in Miami began rounding up organized crime figures from across South Florida. At seventy-one-years of age and with two hip replacements, Charlie Tourine and other aging mobsters answered a subpoena at the Dade County Sheriff's office. Authorities considered Tourine to be one of the most respected mobsters in South Florida. Although he didn't drive because he could hardly read even the simple traffic signs, he was a mastermind when it came to gambling. He had an extensive network of mobbed up associates, and his intimate knowledge of the underworld scene in Miami was one of the reasons police wanted to question him about the Roselli murder. Tourine waxed nostalgic about the old days and freely talked to the deputies about his profession, the casinos he had owned and operated in London, Las Vegas, and Havana. He was also well informed on the plans to bring legalized gambling to Miami as well as his home state of New Jersey. With all his reminiscing, he never said anything

284

about the murder of Johnny Roselli. Charlie Tourine died in May of 1980 at the age of 74.

Joe Nesline

Nesline's guilty plea in his 1986 "VIDGAM" arrest was his last clash with the criminal justice system. Later in his life, during a Washington Post interview with Bob Woodward, Nesline lamented the passing of the old days of gambling in D.C. with $20,000 rolls of the dice. "Gambling, craps, and numbers are at their lowest ebb in Washington," Nesline said wistfully. "The only dice in Washington is in monopoly games." Joseph Francis "Possum" Nesline died in 1995 of natural causes at age 82 living in a Dover, Delaware nursing home.

Addendum

PHOTO

GALLERY

The Foggy Bottom Gang

The Warring Brothers: Leo, Emmett and Charles
(photofrom the book "The Foggy Bottom Gang)
By Leo Warring

Joe Nesline got his start in the underworld with the "Foggy Bottom Gang" as a driver / bootlegger on the "Thunder Road" between Maryland and Washington, D.C. The Warring brothers grew up in the Georgetown section of D.C. where their father ran a cooperage. None of the brothers wanted to continue in the family barrel making business. Bootlegging was easier and more profitable. After prohibition they continued selling untaxed liquor and started running an underground lottery, with reported earnings of $2 million a year.

287

"The Boot," "The Blade" and George Raft

Ruggiero "Richard the Boot" Boiardo (left)
Charlie Tourine and actor George Raft at Boiardo's Livingston, N.J. compound
shortly after Fidel Castro took over the Mob's Capri Casino and Hotel
(photo New Jersey Digest)

Similarities have been pointed out between the life events of Ruggiero Boiardo and Vito Corleone of "The Godfather" movie. Both were orphaned in Italy and came to America in 1901. Both were victims of assassination attempts, they resided in secluded estates, had five children and a son who served in the U.S. armed forces during World War II and became heir of the father's criminal empire. The difference; Vito Corleone is fiction and Sicilian, Ruggiero Boiardo was real and Neapolitan.

"Luigi" the "Bookie"

Louis Prima & Keely Smith
Breaking It Up!
(photo from the album)

Louis Leo "Louie the Lip" Prima and his band, "Prima and his New Orleans Gang" were very popular during the 1930s and 1940s. By the end of the Big-Band era Louis Prima formed his own record label, Robin Hood Records, to release his own material. In 1958, Prima along with his then wife Keely Smith released the album "Breaking It Up." The album featured a song titled "Luigi," the saga of an Italian immigrant "Bookie." A Portion of the lyrics are:

There's a fella named Luigi, he comes from Italy / I wanna be like Luigi 'cause he's always got money.
With a book in his pocket, a pencil in his hand / Luigi's got-a the bees-a-knees that I no understand.
He stand-a on the corner, I think-a he waste his time / People come up to him and say "Number five-a for-a dime."
When you come here, you big-a bum, now you make-a the money by the big-a sum. Now a funny thing-a happen, it happened yesterday / The police-a-man he come and take Luigi far away.
My dear paisano's, I'm telling you, don't be like Luigi or the police-a-man will get you too.

Unlikely Friends

Hyman Chaim aka Harry "Nig Rosen" Stromberg "The Mahoff" (left)
(photo Philadelphia Enquirer)
D.C. Metropolitan Police Major / Superintendent Robert Joseph Barrett (right)
(photo Washington Metropolitan Police Department website)

After the repeal of Prohibition in 1933, the Stromberg mob needed another "Golden Goose," so they pivoted into gambling rackets to make up for lost revenue. They strong-armed their way into partnerships with independent numbers banks and bookmakers like "Jimmy's Place" in D.C. Their message was "Move over because the real gangsters are here now!"

At the time of the Philadelphia gang's incursion into the D.C. area Robert Barrett was a Captain on the D.C. Police force, he was also a friend of "Nig Rosen." Somehow Barrett ascended from the rank of Captain directly to the Chief of Police which was unprecedented.

What is it about Steubenville, Ohio?

Jimmy "The Greek," Dean Martin and Dino Cellini
Steubenville, Ohio, for some reason is the birthplace of a number of famous
individuals in the Casino business.
(photo Gaming Floor: Casino News and Operations Forum)

From the Prohibition Era up until the 1960s, Steubenville was a Mecca for illegal gambling with numerous cigar stores operating as fronts for bookie parlors. The most famous being Rex's Cigar Bar, where Dean Martin, Dino Cellini and Joe Nesline worked for the manager, Cosmo Quattrone. The other cigar shop fronts, just to name a few, are; Capitol Cigar, Corner Cigar, Dixie Cigar, Freddie's, Hy Hat, The Imperial, The Olympic, Penn Lounge, Smokestack and several others. It would seem that Steubenville was the smoking capital of Ohio.

The Burlesque Queens

Josephine Nesline Alvarez (left) at the Merry-Land Club
Heide Reiken (right) at the Blue Mirror
Both clubs were in D.C.
(photo Josephine's book Lucky "325")

Joe Nesline's second wife, Josephine Alvarez was a very popular burlesque star of the 1960s. She performed at clubs from Maine to Miami under the stage name of "Sofina." She appeared along with some of the mainstream entertainers of the day such as "Liberace," the comedy team of "Allen and Rossi" (Marty Allen and Steve Rossi) and others.

The Blue Mirror Club where Heide Reiken performed was also a venue for up-and-coming standup comics including Don Rickles.

292

The Watergate Burglars

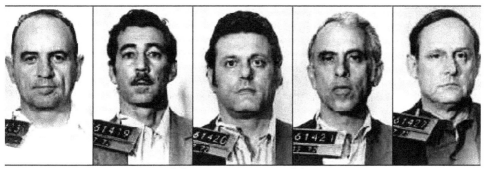

(photo Watergate.Info)

The burglars from left to right

1. James W. McCord, former FBI and CIA agent. Security coordinator for the Republican National Committee (RNC) and Committee for the Re-election of the President (CREEP)
2. Virgilio R. Gonzales, Miami, Florida locksmith and a Cuban refugee
3. Frank A. Sturgis, CIA connections and involvement in Anti-Castro activities
4. Eugenio R. Martinez, CIA connections and involvement in Anti-Castro activities
5. Bernard L. Barker, Miami, Florida Realtor, former CIA operative. Both Sturgis and Martinez were associated with Barker. Martinez worked for Barker's real estate firm

A sixth burglar was former FBI agent and aide for CREEP, Alfred C. Baldwin III. He was in the Howard Johnson Motor Lodge across from the Watergate on surveillance for the entry team in case the police showed up. However, when the police did arrive, he was busy watching "Attack of the Puppet People" on the TV. Baldwin warned the burglars too late. He radioed and said "Well, you've got a problem because there are hippie-looking guys who've got guns."

The Detectives

Sergeant Paul Leeper (left) and Detective John Barrett (right)
Outside the Watergate
(photo Barrett's personal collection)
Detective Carl Schoffler in casual clothes In room 214
of the Watergate Complex during investigation
(photo ABC News)

On Saturday, June 17, 1972 at 2:00 am, the officers answered a call from the dispatcher to investigate a possible break-in at the Watergate complex. They eventually discovered five middle-aged men with Playtex gloves in suits and ties at the Democratic National Committee (DNC) and another person in a room they had rented in a hotel across from the Watergate.

294

The Mob, The Navy and Dewey

The 1948 election of Harry S Truman over
New York Governor Thomas E. Dewey,
would become one of the biggest political upsets in U.S. presidential history
It would forever be memorialized in an embarrassing gaffe in
the Chicago Daily Tribune.

In the late 1940s, rumors were circulated by Dewey's political opponents that he had been bribed to commute Luciano's sentence. In response to the allegations, Governor Dewey asked Judge William B. Herlands to form a commission to look into the entire issue of the Luciano pardon including the question of whether Luciano and his associates provided valuable help to the Navy during WWII. The issue of the Luciano pardon received national attention as part of Senate hearings chaired by Senator Estes Kefauver in 1951.

Judge Herlands' commission finally concluded its inquiry into the Navy-Luciano Affair in September of 1954. The commission found that the Navy Department indeed enlisted the help of the Mob in the war effort and that Luciano's assistance was valuable in securing the New York ports and the invasion of Sicily. The Navy objected to the publication of the full report, and it was not made public for two decades.

295

"Chiri" Mendoza

In 1958, Fulgencio Batista considered the Tryp Habana Hilton
his proudest achievement. Its blue-lit rooftop "Hilton" announced to the world
that Cuba was a safe place in which to invest.
After the Cuban revolution Castro used the hotel as his headquarters
renaming it "Tryp Habana libre"
(photo Blog Melia Cuba)

The Casino in the hotel was leased to a group consisting of Roberto "Chiri" Mendoza, his brother Mario Mendoza, Clifford "Big Juice" Jones among other investors. Many other interested parties were turned down on the lease, one of which was Gambino crime family boss Albert Anastasia. It has been speculated that the murder of Anastasia in 1957, was tied to his interest in securing a stake in the Hilton's Casino. Roberto Mendoza and Santo Trafficante Jr., who had substantial interests in Cuba, were both in New York at the time of Anastasia's murder. Charlie Tourine was also implicated in the murder.

In 1963, a Cuban exile group committed an air bombing on the Cunagua sugar mill in Cuba. The group responsible was the Movimiento Insurreccional de Recuperacion Revolucionaria (MIRR). According to an FBI informant, Roberto "Chiri" Mendoza helped finance MIRR's raid on the sugar mill.

The Corsican Mafia

Marcel Francisi and The "Maure" or the Moor's Head
a symbol of the Unione Corse
The "Maure" is also the Coat of Arms of Corse du Sud,
The southern part of the Island of Corsica
(photo True Crime Detective)

The Unione Corse was a crime syndicate more secretive then the American or Sicilian Mafia. It was made up of Corsican and Italian / French Clans. From the 1950s to the 1970s, they were mainly an international heroin trade network operating between Turkey, Southern France and the United States.

In 1982, Marcel Francisi was assassinated in Paris. He was shot in the head and the heart as he was entering his Jaguar in the parking lot of his apartment building. No motive or suspect was ever firmly established.

Before and After

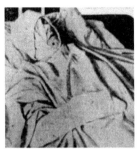

Joe E. Lewis (Joseph Klewan)
(photos My Al Capone Museum)

The above photographs show Singer / Comedian Joe E. Lewis while he was performing at a Chicago Southside club and after he left to work at a Northside club. It was the Southside club's manager, Danny Cohen who asked McGurn to persuade Lewis not to go to the Northside.

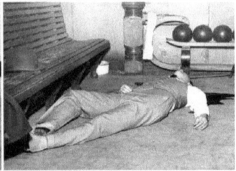

"Machine Gun Jack McGurn" (Vincenzo Antonio Gibaldi)

The above photographs show McGurn when he was a favorite of Al Capone and his Outfit and later, when Capone went to jail, McGurn fell out of favor with Frank Nitti's Outfit.

298

Exiled to Hot Springs

Owen Vincent Madden aka Owney "The Killer " Madden
(photo NYPD mugshot 1931)

Owney Madden was born in Leeds, England and grew up in New York's Hell's Kitchen. He eventually became the leader of a vicious street gang known as the Gopher Gang. He amassed great wealth as a bootlegger and muscling in on night clubs such as the Stork Club. He purchased the Harlem Club DeLuxe from Heavyweight Boxing Champion Jack Johnson and turned it into the famous Cotton Club.

Madden was responsible for multiple murders in New York City. He served time in Sing-Sing for manslaughter. After serving a short prison term for a parole violation, Owney was declared persona-no-grata in New York by prosecutor Thomas Dewey, Mayor Fiorello LaGuardia and Governor Franklin Roosevelt. He was then exiled to the neutral city of Hot Springs, Arkansas where he held court until his death in 1965.

"The Father of Card Counting"

Dr. Edward Oakley Thorp
(photo NEWSWEEK 1964)

After successfully testing his theory on card counting with major syndicate gambler Manny Kimmel in Reno and Las Vegas, Edward Thorp published his 1962 book, "Beat the Dealer." His Ten Count system was the first winning blackjack system ever made public for beating any major casino gambling game. When Thorp's book became a best-seller, the Las Vegas casinos switched from dealing hand-held one-deck games to four-deck shoe games. In 1966 Thorp's revised second edition of "Beat the Dealer" was published which had a High-Low Count, a more practical counting system for attacking the new shoe games.

Geniuses

Steve Wozniak (left) and Steve Jobs (right)
(photo New Atlas)

Prior to founding Apple computer in 1976, Wozniak and Jobs had a brief and highly illegal business manufacturing the world's first digital phone hacking tool known as the "Blue Box." In 2017 a complete Wozniak-Jobs "Blue Box" sold for $125,000 at Bonhams' History of Science and Technology sale.

The original "Blue Box" on display in the Computer History Museum
in Mountain View, California

"Genius on Hold"

Walter L. Shaw (left) the inventor of the "Black Box"
Inspiration for the Wozniak-Jobs "Blue Boxes"
Son Walter T. Shaw (right) former Luchese crime family soldier
(photo BYTEWRITER.COM)

Father and son were estranged from each other until they finally reconciled thanks to the son's wife. The son spent 11 years in a Florida Correctional Institution. After serving his time the younger Shaw had a face-to-face meeting with John Gotti and resigned as a "Soldato" (soldier) in the Mob. According to Shaw it is called "going on the shelf."

"Lucky Lefty"

Frank "Lefty" Rosenthal, one of Joe Nesline's many associates
Adjusts his tie while refusing to answer questions at
Senate Subcommittee hearings Washington, D.C.
September 7, 1961

A fortunate manufacturing flaw in "Lefty's" 1981 Cadillac Eldorado
allowed him to survive an assassination attempt on October 4, 1982
outside Las Vegas' Tony Roma's restaurant
(photo Las Vega Review-Journal Archive)

"Jersey Boys"

Nigerian Light-heavyweight Champion Dick Tiger versus Frankie DePaula
Madison Square Garden, October 25, 1968
(photo Ring Magazine "Fight of the Year")

Anthony "Gary" Garafola (left)
Leaving Manhattan criminal court, May 28, 1969
James "Jimmy Nap" Napoli (right)
At Madison Square Garden
(photo the BUTTONGUYS)

The M&M Murders

The infamous case of the 1962 Chicago M&M murders was depicted in the 1995 Martin Scorsese movie Casino.

The Victims

Jimmy Miraglia (left) and Billy McCarthy (right)
(photo Chicago Tribune)

The Perps

Anthony "The Ant" Spilatro (left) ordered the murders
Frank John Cullotta (center) gave them up
Charles Anthony Nicoletti (right) along with "Milwaukee Phil" Alderisio
Carried out the murders
(photos WGN9 Chicago, Las Vegas Sun and FAMOUSFIX respectively)

About the Author

Angelo Parisi is a retired Detective from the Metropolitan Police Department of Washington, D.C. with 25 years of service. Most of his career was spent in the Intelligence Division with detailed assignments to federal task forces with the FBI, U.S. Secret Service, U.S. Marshals Service and INTERPOL. Since retirement in 2003, he has been a federal contractor with the FBI's international drug squad and Director of Security for a D.C. based lobbying firm as well as security gigs with national and international news outlets. In 2012 he appeared in an episode of a documentary television series on the Biography Channel, Gangsters: America's Most Evil, The Mayor of Harlem: Alberto "Alpo" Martinez.

Bibliography

Books

A Heartbeat Away:
The Investigation and Resignation of Vice President Spiro T. Agnew
By Richard Cohen and Jules Witcove

A License To Steal
By Walter T. Shaw

Beat the Dealer
By Edward O. Thorp

Charles "The Blade" Tourine: Genovese Capo-Regime
By Robert Grey Reynolds Jr.

The Chronicles of The Last Jewish Gangster: From Myer to Myron
By Myron Sugarman

THE CORPORATION: An epic story of the Cuban American Underworld
By T.J. English

The Crime Buff's Guide To Outlaw Washington, D.C.
By Ron Franscell

Deep Politics and the Death of JFK
By Dale Scott

Fish Rain Coats: A Woman Lawyer's Life
By Barbara Babcock

The Foggy Bottom Gang: The Story of the Warring Brothers of Washington, D.C

By Leo Warring

Fortune's Formula:
The Untold Story of the Scientific Betting System
That Beat the Casinos and Wall Street
By William Poundstone

Freddie Foreman: The Godfather of British Crime
By Freddie Foreman

Gangsterismo: The United States, Cuba and the Mafia
By Jack Colhoun

Havana Nocturne
By T. J. English

The Hollywood Connection:
The Mafia and the movie business-the explosive story
By Michael Munn

INTERFERANCE: How Organized Crime Influences Professional Football
By Dan Moldea

JERSEY BOY
By Adeyinka Makinde

Lucky 325
By Josephine Nesline Alvarez
MAFIALAND: How the Mob Invaded Britain
By Douglas Thompson

MAFIA ALLIES:
The True Story of America's Secret Alliance with the Mob in World War II
By Tim Newark

Master of the Game: Steve Ross and the Creation of Time Warner

By Connie Bruck

MASTERS of PARADISE:
Organized crime and the Internal Revenue Service in the Bahamas
By Alan A. Block

Nixon's Secrets
By Roger Stone with Mike Colapietro

Organized Crime
By Howard Abadinsky

The Organized Crime Community
Essays in Honor of Alan A. Block,
Edited by Frank Bovenkerk and Michael Levi

The Politics of Heroin in Southeast Asia:
The Mafia comes to Asia, Santo Trafficante visited Saigon in 1968
By Alfred W. McCoy

Prohibition in Washington, D.C.: How Dry We Weren't
by Garrett Peck

Secret Agenda: Watergate, Deep Throat and the CIA
By Jim Hougan

Shoot Out At Jackson City
By George Axiotis

Silent Coup
By Len Colodny & Robert Gettlin

Some Unpopular History of the United States: The Richard Nixon Years
Jan. 1969 – Aug. 9, 1974
By Richard McManus

Washington Confidential
By Jack Lait & Lee Mortimer

WHEN VICE WAS KING: A HISTORY OF NORTHERN KENTUCKY GAMBLING
1920-1970
By Jim Linduff with Roy Klein & Larry Trapp

White House Call Girl: The Real Watergate Story
By Phil Stanford

Wicked Northern Virginia
By Michael Lee Pope

Newspaper and Magazine Articles

The Baltimore Sun / Middleman Agnew does it his way AGNEW: After the Fall
March 07, 1993 / By Dan Fesperman

Chicago Times / Irwin Weiner Witnessed Dorfman `Hit'
June 05, 1996/ By John O'Brien

The Evening Star / Warring Holdup Pressed Despite Denials
January 12, 1950 / Bulletin

The Evening Star / Warring Holup Search Centers on Ex-Friends
January 13, 1950 / Bulletin

The Evening Star / Stromberg Identified by Warring Maid in $24,000 Robbery
April 4, 1950 / Bulletin

The Evening Star / Gambler Slain in Gun Attack at After-Hours Club
January 10, 1951 / Bulletin

The Evening Star / Nesline Murder Trial Expected to Continue
April 14, 1951 / Bulletin

The Evening Star / Holtzoff Indicates Nesline Murder Trial Will Go to Jury Today
April 18, 1951 / By Charles J. Yarbrough

The Evening Star / Nesline Freed in Slaying Gets Year for Gun
April 19, 1951 / By Charles J. Yarbrough

The Evening Star / Knew Harding, Stromberg says but denies Warring Holup
September 12, 1951 / By John W, Stepp

The Evening Star / Nesline raid failure scrutinized
July 22, 1959 / By George Kennedy

Executive Intelligence Review / Carter Candidates For FBI Chief Are Fabians
In Conservative Clothing
July 5, 1977 / By Marilyn James

The Frederick Post / Gangland link eyed in Montgomery death
August 12,1976 / By Ruth W. Johnson

The Hoya, Georgetown University News Paper / The "Dry" History of D.C.
June 22, 2015 / By Blair Kennedy

Jet Magazine / Ella, Sinatra, Basie, Quincy Jones Send Inmates
July 29, 1965 / Entertainment section

Las Vegas Review-Journal / Bob Martin
February 7, 1999 / By A.D. Hopkinslas

Las Vegas Sun / Pioneer casino exec, dealers school owner Ayoub dies at 77
August 27, 2001

Life Magazine / The Scandal of the Bahamas
February 3, 1967 / By Richard Oulahan & William Lambert

National Review / Alcee Hastings, Bribery, and the House Intelligence Committee
November 17, 2006 / By Byron York

The New York Times / Kerkorian is Named at Crime Hearing
September 28, 1971 / By Nicholas Gage

The New York Times / Kerkorian's Name Is Brought In
As Crime Inquiry Hears Tape
January 17, 1979 / By Thomas F Brady

The New York Times / Collapse Of Deak & Company
By Nicholas D. Kristof / December 10, 1984

The New York Times / G.O.P. Hopeful Facing Problems in Bid for
Michigan Governorship
September 26, 1985 / By Phil Gailey

Richmond Times-Dispatch / Man gets life sentence for 1969 murder
June 1, 2007 / By Matthew Barakat, The Associated Press

Regardie Magazine / Jimmy's Place
1987 / By Frank Kuznick

The Saratogian / Beirut Casino
February 22, 1964

Seattle Post Intelligencer / Former CIA spy branded a traitor
wants to clear his name
October 22, 2006 / By Tracy Johnson

South Florida Sun Sentinel / Romano Dies; Prominent in Hastings Case
October 20, 1985 / By Katie Springer

South Florida Sun Sentinel / The Gangster Next Door
September 24, 1989 / By Larry Keller

Sports Illustrated / Mr. Jim made a million from a casino brooking no booze, women of guns
October 11, 1976 / By Charles Price

Tampa Bay Times / From paints to Paradise Island
September 27, 2005 / By Robert Trigaux

Tampa Mafia / Mobsters, Libations & Stogies / Washington DC's
Most Notorious Gambler
Fall 2014, Volume 1 / Issue 1 / By Jack Calhoun

The Telegraph UK Newspaper / Boxer Freddie Mills was murdered by the Mob
July 28, 2018 / By Anita Singh

UPI / Grandma Mafia Ringleader Faces Life In Prison
May 4, 1983

Washingtonian / The only kind of Washington Lawyer that's gone extinct
August 18, 2015 / By Britt Peterson

The Washington Post / Criminal Activity of Shocking Enormity
Revealed Thriving in Nation's Capital
May 3, 1951 / By Douglas Larsen

The Washington Post / The Mafia's Ties in Convention City (Miami)
July 1972 / By Jack Anderson

The Washington Post / Agnew Told of "Terrible" Pressure
April 19, 1974 / By Jack Anderson

The Washington Post / Tongsun Park's Club
October 16, 1977 / By Phil McCombs

The Washington Post / D.C. Gambling Kingpin Is Linked
To Prominent Investors' Casino Deal
January 26, 1978 / By Maxine Cheshire, contributors Robin Groom,

Amy Nathan & Shelley Zucker.

The Washington Post / Bobrow, Linked to Narcotics,
Found Shot Dead in Apartment
December 13, 1978

The Washington Post / Bagley Accuses the Post, Reporter Of Bias
in Printing Casino Story
January 28, 1978 / By Stephen J. Lynton

The Washington Post / Policemen Seized in Confidence Game
May 30, 1979 / By Ron Shaffer & Alfred E. Lewis

The Washington Post / Man Charged in Scheme Here
Found Slain in Las Vegas Home
October 12, 1979 / By Timothy S. Robinson

The Washington Post / "Whitetop" Simkins' Son Acquitted of Taking Bets
November 7, 1980 / By Joe Pichirallo

The Washington Post / Joseph Nesline Jailed for Contempt in Hastings Case
December 4, 1981 / By Janis Johnson

The Washington Post / Washingtonian Is Arrested on Gambling Charges
December 15, 1981 / By Alfred E. Lewis

The Washington Post / Deak-Perera Chairman Fatally Shot in Office
November 19, 1985 / By Margot Hornblower

The Washington Post / D.C. Rackets Figure Nesline Pleads Guilty in Video Case
January 24, 1987 / By Nancy Lewis

The Washington Post / With the Mafia Muscling in,
We Soon May Long for the Bad Old Days
March 1, 1987 / By Nancy Lewis

The Washington Post / The Perplexing Case of Judge Alcee Hastings
July 7, 1988 / By Marjorie Williams

The Washington Post / The Day it Poured
February 27, 1994 / By Linda Wheeler

The Washington Post / Celebrated D.C. Restaurateur Duke Zeibert Dies at 86
August 16, 1997 / By Bart Barnes

The Washington Post / Getting Down to Business With Landow
April 6, 1998 / By Peter Carlson

The Washington Post Magazine / AKA FRANK SINATRA
March 7, 1999 / By Jeff Leen

The Washington Post / Donald A. Brew says he killed a woman in 1969
after she testified against him before a grand jury
March 7, 2007 / By Rich Lipski & Theresa Vargas

Blogs

Arlington Fire Journal & Metro D.C. Fire History / Jackson City
June 25, 2009 / By Vinny Del Giudice

Bahamas Hoodlum Sea - Jabez Corner / Bahamian Fragments, Bits and Pieces
from the History of The Bahamas; Bahamas Hoodlum Sea, The Grim Reapers
By Ed Reid

Boundary Stones / WETA's Local History Blog / Jackson City:
Arlington 's Monte Carlo
October 6, 2017 / By Callum Cleary

Boundary Stones / WETA's Local History Blog / Washington's Godfather
"Gentleman Gambler" Jimmy Lafontaine
October 10, 2017 / By Callum Cleary

Coffee or Die Magazine /The Rise and Fall of Odessa Madre, "The Lady Al Capone"
February 27, 2019 / By Matt Fratus

Cosa Nostra News / Fat Tony: A Mobster's Mobster to the End
March 21, 2011 / By Ed Scarpa

Cosa Nostra News / Milwaukee Phil Drove a "Hitmobile" Too
July 21, 2014 / By Ed Scarpa

Gaming floor / CASINO NEWS & OPERATIONS FORUM /
What is it about Steubenville, Ohio?
June 25, 2012

Gangster Inc, / The Italian Mafia in the Netherlands
January 15, 2007 / By David Ambrose

Gangster Inc, / Man is the Cruelest Animal:
The True Story of "Trigger Mike" Coppola
June 5, 2011 / By Thom L. Jones

The Gangster Report / The Possum and the President:
JFK Partied With Mob on Inauguration Day '61, Led to His Shunning the Rat Pack
December 2, 2021 / By Scott Burnstein

History Daily / So That's Why They're Called Hookers
August 25, 2019

IMASPORTSPHILE / Sports Comedy Music Index
Music – 1974 – Frank Sinatra – My Way

International Boxing Research Organization (IBRO) /
BOB FOSTER: THE BORGER BANGER
Boxing Biographies
March 26, 2012 / By Austin Killeen

Intrepid Report.com / The tragic ends of the CIA's madams
December 18, 2014 / By Wayne Madsen

Investigative Notes / Hougan, Liddy, The Post and Watergate
June 22, 2011

LewRockwell.com / It's the 40th Anniversary of the Watergate Conspiracy
June 16, 2012 / By Charles Burris

MAFIA WIKI /Carlos Marcello / Dino Cellini / Santo Trafficante Jr.

Mental Floss / (9) Things You Didn't Know Where Paid for by a Lottery
January 11, 2016 / By Kevin Flynn

THE MOB MUSEUM / Jack Ruby and telephone calls to Mobsters:
Evidence of a JFK conspiracy?
By Gerald Posner

Rick Porrello's American Mafia.com / The Blade
September 13, 2016 / By Scott M. Deitche

THE MOB MUSEUM / Rose Marie: At Home With "Uncle Al"
November 30, 2017 / By Marcy Knight

My Al Capone Museum / Joe E. Lewis (and The Green Mill)

Quixotic Joust / Off The Boards / Gil Beckley / Heidi Rikan
March 30, 2011

THE RAKE, THE MODERN VOICE OF CLASSIC ELEGANCE /
RAKISH DYNASTIES: JOE AND JOHN F KENNEDY
The story of this American establishment dynasty's rise is so good, it's criminal
May 2016 / By Christian Barker

Reddit / Who Killed Freddie Mills?
Suspicious Death in the Heart of Swinging Sixties London

September 2020

RelicRecord.com / General Hooker's Sweet Bella Hay
April 1, 2019

Salon /James Bond and the killer Bag Lady
New clues and a powerful Wall St. skeptic
challenge the official story of CIA financier Nick Deak's brutal murder
December 2, 2012 / By Mark James – Alexander Zaitchik

Spartacus Educational / American History / The Assassination of JFK /
Bobby Baker
September 1997 / By John Simkin

Spartacus Educational / American History / Disinformation / I. Irving Davidson
September 1997 / By John Simkin

The STONEZONE / Agnew Hooked on Meth
November 11, 2014

UPI Archive / MIAMI -- Reputed underworld kingpins Santos Trafficante and
Anthony 'Big Tuna' Accardo and 13 others pleaded innocent to federal
racketeering indictments returned by a grand jury at Miami
June 19, 1981

Washington D.C. Metropolitan Police Memorial and Museum
Memorial to Francis M. Doyle
Washington Post Article
March 19, 1911 / Transcribed by David Richardson (MPDC Ret.)

Wednesday-Night / Where the world comes together August 1960,
The Unique and Meaningful LORTON JAZZ FESTIVAL
December 21, 1991 / By Diana Thebaud Nicholso

Government Records

United States of America Congressional Record
Proceedings and Debates of the 82nd Congress, First Session /
Volume 97, Part 3 Page 3115
March 27, 1951 to April 25, 1951

United States of America Congressional Record
Proceedings and Debates of the 82nd Congress, First Session /
Volume 97, Part 4
April 26, 1951 to May 24, 1951

FBI Report CR 63-7893-9
Subject: Irwin Sidney Weiner, James Riddle Hoffa
November 15, 1962

FBI Report CR 63-8306-14
Subject: James Plumeri, Irwin Sidney Weiner
June 21, 1963

FBI Report 166-637-20
Subject: Charles Tourine, Joseph Francis Nesline
July 17, 1963

President's Commission on the Assassination of President Kennedy
and the Death of Lee Harvey Oswald
August 14, 1964 / Testimony of Lawrence V. Meyers

FBI Report 92-2989-222
Subject: Charles Tourine
January 13, 1965

FBI Reprt 92-2831-B

Subject: Meyer Lansky Group
August 11, 1967

FBI Report 62-71692-2
Subject: Edward K. Moss
December 15, 1969

FBI Report 92-2989-253
Subject: Charles Tourine
December 23, 1969

United States Senate 93rd Congress / Organized Crime Securities:
Thefts and Frauds
Hearings before the Permanent Subcommittee on Investigations / PART 2
September 18 and 19, 1973 / Sworn Testimony of Louis Pasquale Mastriana

FBI Report 87-126535-15
Subject: Irwin Sidney Weiner
July 16, 1974

House Select Committee on Assassinations (HSCA) 180-101117-10032
Subject: Anti-Castro Activity; Carrafo, Eugene Michael; Roselli, John;
Organized Crime; Oswald, Lee Harvey; CIA
August 2, 1976

Naval Intelligence and the Mafia in World War II
By Rear Admiral Tom Burke, USN (ret.)

House of Representatives Senate Committee on Assassinations,
JFK Subcommittee Hearing
[Executive Session] Washington, D.C.
May 18, 1978 / Testimony of Irwin Sidney Weiner

United States House of Representatives / House Select Committee
On Assassinations
United States Federal Building / U.S. Magistrate Courtroom 16-F23 /

Dallas, Texas
May 22, 1978 / Sworn Testimony of Joseph Campisi

Nova Law Review
Volume 19 Issue 3 Article 2
The Curious Case of Alcee Hastings
1995 / By Alan I. Brown

United States Congressional Record /
Senate Impeachment Trial Committee Hearings On Articles of Impeachment
Against Judge Alcee L. Hastings, A Judge of the United States District Court for
the Southern District of Florida For High Crimes and Misdemeanors /
Part 2B of 3 Parts
July 27, 1989 to August 22, 1989

United States Court of Appeals, Fourth Circuit
Ida Maxwell Wells, Plaintiff Appellant, v. G. Gordan Liddy, Defendant –
Appellee, Phillip Mackin Bailley, Movant No. 98-1962
Decided July 28, 1999

Printed in the USA
CPSIA information can be obtained
at www.ICGtesting.com
CBHW051118021223
2299CB00007B/177